Praise fo[illegible]Dream

"Dale speaks with authority and will remin[illegible] of a simple truth: your dreams are worth chasing. Inside *Launch Your Dream*, he lays out a blueprint that removes the guesswork for turning your calling into your career. In following Dale's plan, you will overcome your fears; be excited to chase your dreams; and in the process, transform not just your work, but also your life."

—Mark Burnett, creator of ABC's *Shark Tank*

"Starting a business is tough—no doubt about it. But getting stuck in a *j-o-b* that doesn't feed your dreams and passions can be so much worse! Dale Partridge gives entrepreneurs the practical tools they need to escape that rut and successfully live out their calling in life."

—Dave Ramsey, bestselling author and
nationally syndicated radio show host

"*Launch Your Dream* provides an easy-to-follow, finely tuned framework to enable anyone to identify their calling, do what they love, and love what they do. It's a get-out-of-jail-free pass for those languishing in their day jobs and the recipe for purpose many are starving for. At the core, the principles on these pages will save you countless hours trying to figure 'it' out on your own. Instead, steal back the control of your life . . . for good."

—John J. Kilcullen, creator of the
For Dummies™ book series

"When it comes to launching a new business, for many people, it's the start that stops them. If you dream about doing something more, something different, something that inspires you, then this book is for you. Dale Partridge's new book, *Launch Your Dream*, will motivate and equip you with the practical tools to turn your dream into a reality. This book will not only help you succeed at what you do professionally—it will help you succeed in every area of your life."

—Craig Groeschel, author and
founder of Life.Church

LAUNCH YOUR DREAM

LAUNCH YOUR DREAM

A 30-DAY PLAN FOR TURNING YOUR PASSION INTO YOUR PROFESSION

DALE PARTRIDGE

HarperCollins Leadership

An Imprint of HarperCollins

Published by HarperCollins Leadership, an imprint of HarperCollins Focus LLC.

Author is represented by The Christopher Ferebee Agency, www.christopherferebee.com.

ISBN: 978-0-7180-9341-9 (HC)
ISBN: 978-0-7180-9342-6 (eBook)
ISBN: 978-1-4002-0826-5 (TP)
ISBN: 978-0-7180-9895-7 (ITPE)

Library of Congress Cataloging-in-Publication Data

Names: Partridge, Dale, 1985-author.
Title: Launch your dream: a 30-day plan for turning your passion into your profession / Dale Partridge.
Description: Nashville, Tennessee: Nelson Books, [2017]
Identifiers: LCCN 2016044237 | ISBN 9780718093419
Subjects: LCSH: New business enterprises. | Business planning. | Small business—Management. | Entrepreneurship.
Classification: LCC HD62.5 .P378 2017 | DDC 658.1/1—dc23 LC record available at https://lccn.loc.gov/2016044237

Printed in the United States of America

19 20 21 22 23 LSC 6 5 4 3 2 1

To Aria—your little soul is a big force behind my work. I hope having a father who chases his dreams will motivate you to chase yours.

Contents

0

You Were Made for This

I remember getting out of bed after a night of not sleeping. The ghost of insomnia had been haunting my house for months. Most nights I managed to find at least an hour of shut-eye, but not this night. Not even a wink. I'd spent the night staring at the ceiling, tossing from side to side, trying without success to will myself to sleep. This was becoming all too familiar.

Each morning, after the specter of insomnia faded, the demon of anxiety arrived to torment me. *How will I pay my bills? How will I pay my employees? How will I find time to be a good husband?* Questions swirled in my mind, often leaving me paralyzed. I was overstressed, overworked, overloaded.

From the outside, I was the picture of success. I had founded a multimillion-dollar e-commerce company that was growing like kudzu. But along with the wins there were new weights and responsibilities. The fifty-some employees working in my company's Costa Mesa headquarters required $300,000 of monthly revenue just to sustain the payroll. Over time, walking into the office felt like serving out a prison sentence—and I wasn't sure there was the possibility of parole. My passion for the day-to-day operations began to wane as I realized that I hadn't fulfilled my dream; I had created a job.

The worry of it all eventually manifested in physical symptoms—not just insomnia, but muscle twitching, acute acid reflux, and difficulty breathing. I finally decided to reach out to a physician friend, who informed me that I wasn't sick; I was stuck. Living in Los Angeles had taken its toll—the noise, the lights, the traffic jams, the poor air quality, the threat of violent crime. The city was a constant bombardment of energy that overstimulated my mind and body. And worse, it had begun to affect my wife, Veronica. Her nervousness had risen to a point of near debilitation. She hadn't left the house in weeks, too anxious to get into the car and drive to the job she had come to loathe.

After a particularly torturous day at the office, I sulked my way into our house and found Veronica looking at me with desperation. "We've got to get out of here," she said.

I couldn't disagree. She was right. The pressures of our life in a sprawling, smoggy city had become unsustainable for both of us. Where had it all gone wrong? In 2012, in the spirit of the 1849 gold rushers, I had moved to Orange County, California. Opportunity was budding. I started my first businesses in an effort to free myself from the corporate dungeon that had trapped so many of my friends. But along the way, the very thing I was trying to escape had imprisoned me. My body, my mind, and now my wife were all telling me it was time to leave.

A few nights after Veronica confessed her desire to escape the city, I finally stole an hour of sleep. I dreamed I was walking in a field at the base of a beautiful mountain range with my wife in front of me. She was holding the hand of a small girl—a child whom I did not yet know—and both of them were wearing cowboy boots. I didn't know where this place was, but when my eyes blinked open, I longed to discover it.

The dream rolled around in my head day after day, until a Facebook algorithm was changed. Then everything shifted. Because my e-commerce company had been built on the back of social media marketing, the Facebook changes threatened to destroy it. My board reacted by "deciding to take the company in a new direction"—and in that plan, they felt I was no longer necessary.[1] When the shock of the news dissipated, I realized the loss was actually a gift. In that moment, the trays on the scale of my life shifted and moving seemed the only logical next step. As author Henry Cloud said, "We change our behavior when the pain of staying the same becomes greater than the pain of changing."[2]

With the tether to my company severed, I was now free to look for that field from my dream and take my family there. The search began, and within a year, we had sold our house in California and moved to Bend, Oregon. The insomnia dissolved, the anxiety dispersed, and the acid reflux dissipated. And Veronica and I found the parcel of land where we could build our family farm and realize our dreams.

Sometimes people tell me I'm crazy for leaving one of the biggest, sexiest cities in the greatest country on earth to move to a small town in Central Oregon with very little industry to speak of and two hours from a major airport. Why would Veronica and I give up seemingly endless opportunities in Los Angeles for this kind of life, where our livelihood depends on our ability to launch and sustain a new company? Why wouldn't we just settle down and work for a stable Fortune 500 company with a strong benefits package and 401(k)?

Whenever someone questions why we made this decision, I always reply, "Because we were made for this."

Since the Beginning

Business historians began to study entrepreneurship in the early part of the twentieth century, though the word *entrepreneur* first emerged in the colonial era. But the history of entrepreneurship actually begins with the dawn of time. Unlike in the famous GEICO advertising campaign, we have no records of cavemen wearing suits or "working for the man." When God created the first humans, they survived as hunters and foragers who had to find ways to provide for their families using their ingenuity, sweat, and sharpened sticks. They didn't have bosses. No one did.

The Neolithic revolution gave rise to an agricultural society with permanent settlements and social classes. But somehow, entrepreneurship still reigned. People worked the land to feed themselves and their loved ones. If one year's harvest was particularly bountiful, farmers might trade their extra produce to others for something they needed. As communities banded together to exchange excess goods, markets formed. And this gave rise to a new creature: the merchant. These self-employed individuals were especially gifted at selling, bartering, and trading. They dreamed up new ways to make profits using goods created by someone else who existed farther up the supply chain.

Then the world shifted yet again. In 1602, the Dutch East India Company became a chartered company and, according to most historians, the first multinational corporation in history. They were the first business to sell and issue stocks to investors, which led to exponential expansion. The Dutch East India Company soon dominated the global spice trade—until it imploded almost two hundred years later due to widespread corporate corruption. (I'm sure you're shocked.) But while the company went belly up, its legacy remained. Other businesses began mimicking its behavior, attempting to build corporations that rivaled modest-sized governments.

The twentieth century saw the culmination of the industrial revolution and the dawn of the information age, which together propelled us to a frontier never before traveled by human beings. In our current era, personal freedom and self-employment are often sacrificed on the altar of new virtues, like balance and stability. Think about Cornelius Vanderbilt, John D. Rockefeller, and Andrew Carnegie. Was anything about their lives balanced or stable? No. And yet they accomplished great feats in transportation, energy, and construction. But today, anything imbalanced or unstable feels dangerous. The entrepreneurial life is neither of these. And that's part of what makes it exciting.

Most people in the developed world work for corporations, both large and small. We forget too easily that employment is a relatively new concept in human history. Ever since the first fig-leaf-covered humans walked the earth, entrepreneurship has been the predominant way people have made money and provided for their families. So when I tell people who question my move that "we were made for this," I am not just referring to Veronica and me. I mean most humans throughout history. And maybe even most humans today.

How do I know that so many people were made to start their own businesses? Because many people who are trying the other option are flat-out miserable.

A National Epidemic

If 70 percent of Americans woke up with polio tomorrow, we would call it a national epidemic. But 70 percent of Americans say they wake up every day dissatisfied with their current jobs, and somehow there is no outcry.[3] By our own accounts, we are witnessing a national epidemic of job dissatisfaction.

If stress is defined as working hard at something you dislike, then tens of millions of Americans are on their way toward a career-based nervous breakdown. Forty million Americans now suffer from anxiety, and roughly sixty million suffer from insomnia or another sleep disorder. Too many of us are underpaid and overworked, beat up by our bosses and burned out by our duties. We want more purpose, more time with our loved ones, more freedom over our schedules. We want to love what we do and do what we love.

As a result, we are now witnessing the demise of the nine to five, the death of passionless work, and the end of an employment mind-set that is fixated on fulfilling other people's dreams. There has been a seismic shift toward self-employment on both sides of the Atlantic. In Britain, 90 percent of the new jobs created in the fourth quarter of 2013 were classed as self-employment. And in the United States, 74 percent of new jobs in 2014 were classed the same way. Since 2008, we've seen a structural shift in how culture views job security. Tens of millions of people, from college students to retirees, are choosing to work for themselves rather than donating their loyalty to another j-o-b. The future, it seems, belongs to the self-employed.

Not everyone is moving their family from a bustling metropolis to Central Oregon—and not everyone should—but they are making decisions to stop suffering and start starting. They've discovered what I learned a long time ago: if you don't chase your dreams, someone will hire you to build theirs.

Helping Starters Start

After relocating, Veronica and I decided that part of our dream was to help other people realize theirs. When we wed, Veronica and I had $40,000 in combined debt and made less than that per year. I was between jobs, and Veronica was a dog groomer at PetSmart. But I realized over time that I was made to be an entrepreneur. So I became a serial starter, birthing more than half a dozen companies—from a rock-climbing gym to a branding agency to my e-commerce company. Some were launched well and others poorly, but each one taught me valuable lessons about how to start and run a business.

I've learned that one of the first steps to realizing your dreams is identifying your gifts. In Oregon, I began accepting that I'm good at chasing dreams. I have a unique talent for seeing a desirable future and transforming it into reality. I have benefited from this gift over the years, and now I want to help others do the same.

I looked back at my history—the wins and losses—and recorded all the lessons I'd learned. I surveyed the most successful innovators and influencers I knew to gather their best practices. I wanted to help people create businesses that would last. To locate my blind spots and help people save time, I asked myself questions I hadn't asked in years:

- How do I know what I really enjoy doing?
- How do I determine what my purpose is?
- How do I create a product that excites and empowers others?
- How do I build a compelling brand and online presence?

I returned to the basics, shoring up the foundations of my business philosophy. And then I crafted a curriculum with a step-by-step process to launch a successful business into an online course. We may already be verging on the death of traditional education. A four-year investment and $80,000 is no longer appealing for everyone seeking to strike out on their own. Instead, many are turning toward self-learning through at-your-own-pace resources. Future entrepreneurs need affordable, accessible tools to turn their ideas into a profitable reality. A twelve-month online course began to make the most sense. As the proverbial lightbulb flickered, StartupCamp was born.

More than a thousand participants enrolled in StartupCamp the first year—from millennial innovators to stay-at-home parents to recent retirees looking to start a twilight career. The course encouraged "campers" to begin launching their businesses in the first six months. Success stories poured out:

- Jesse started a brewery outside of Seattle. It's a tap house that specializes in gourmet bar food. Every drink purchased helps provide clean water to a child in need.
- Brady started a wedding photography business in Southern California. He's making a six-figure salary snapping beautiful pictures of happy couples.
- Jessica launched a coffee-roasting company in Texas. She decided to make organic, fair-trade coffee that valued people over profit. (She ended up making a nice profit too.)
- Jack started a blog, podcast, and YouTube channel from his home in Copenhagen, Denmark. These media now generate income for Jack and his wife.
- Hector and Nancy launched a design agency in Pomona, California. They specialize in minimalist but gorgeous web design.
- Jillian was already a business consultant who had begun an online stationery company based in Dallas. Thanks to StartupCamp, her revenue has increased tenfold and her work has been featured on the *Huffington Post*, *Domino*, and other major online publications.

- Two brothers, Nicholas and Lucas, started an outdoor gear company and online journal based in Pennsylvania. They donate a portion of their profit to fund conservation efforts.

But what about all those people who aren't ready to commit twelve months to StartupCamp? That's where this book comes in. In your hands, you hold an abridged version that can be completed in just thirty days. That's right. To begin turning your passion into a profession, all you need to commit to is one month.

Find Your Farm

Veronica and I have finally moved into our farmhouse nestled on seven acres outside Bend, Oregon. The backyard is a field where my wife often walks hand in hand with our daughter, Aria. Sometimes they wear cowboy boots. Next to the field is a pen where our miniature donkey, Diego, can be found braying. A trinity of mountains collectively known as the Three Sisters—charity, hope, and faith—rise up in the distance. Each night when I watch the purplish sunset against that backdrop and consider the dream I'm living, I'm reminded that we humans are homesick for a more truthful existence. But before we can come home, we must shatter the myths we've allowed to infiltrate our minds.

When you work for someone else, you assume you're secure. But you aren't. You could be fired tomorrow because of someone else's bad decision. When you work for someone else, you assume you are in control of your life. But you aren't. You're at the mercy of someone you *think* you know, but probably don't. When you work for someone else, you assume you're pursuing success. But you aren't. There is no greater failure than missing out on what you were made to do.

In addition to releasing these myths, you may need to let go of the idea that entrepreneurship is a get-rich-quick scheme. While we all long to live a life of depth and meaning, we often pursue the emptiness of fame and fortune. Everyone needs to make enough money to survive, and many who complete this thirty-day journey will go on to amass enormous wealth. But most will start out working more hours and earning less money than they might otherwise. The wages of self-employment are not dollars and cents, but freedom and purpose.

Costless success doesn't exist. A cost had to be paid when we left the city. I no longer have access to as many people as I once did. I'm no longer invited to parties with the famous and fabulous. But the price we've paid to live our dream is lower than the dividends it is paying out to our family. You may feel your pockets are empty and you don't have the capital to invest in your dreams. Let me be up front: Launching a dream is not for everyone, and it may not be for you.

If your goal in life is to buy a Lamborghini . . . then this book is not for you.

If your goal in life is to be "known" by a million strangers . . . then this book is not for you.

If your goal in life is to support other people's visions . . . then this book is not for you.

But . . .

If you believe that you don't have to be smarter to be a starter . . . then this book is for you.

If you believe that meaning trumps money . . . then this book is for you.

If you believe that everything worth having is worth paying a price for . . . then this book is for you.

Not everyone is meant to work for themselves. But if you sense the ancient spirit of the entrepreneur stirring inside of you and have an inkling that you might be ready to act on it, then let's begin the journey together.

Launching a dream doesn't have to be complicated. So in the pages that follow, you'll discover short chapters with estimated reading times posted at the top. Time is an important asset, and I want to help you plan for this journey. At the end of each day, you'll discover four opportunities to interact with what you just learned.

1. The "Remember" statements are quotes and poetic phrases that will help remind you who you are and what you are trying to accomplish.
2. The "Ask" questions will help you think about how the material specifically relates to your dream.
3. The "Believe" statements are written in the first person because they are meant to focus you on a principle you'll need to weave into your life in order to succeed. Post them on your walls; recite them in your mind; own them in your life.
4. The "Do" assignments will help you take tangible steps toward your launch. You might not be able to finish every assignment in a single day, but that's okay. This book leads you on a thirty-day journey of learning. But because our dreams vary, the time it will take you to launch may also vary.

As for Veronica and me, we left that city and we built that farm. We chased that dream, and we found our freedom. We've built the life we've always wanted—and you can do the same. A more truthful existence awaits you.

Get Ready

DAY 1

Primed with Passion

Estimated Reading Time: 8 Minutes

The idea that "you should do what you're passionate about" is so common in modern business literature that it has become almost annoying. Yet most of us still recognize it as true. Sure, working with passion is a first-world luxury—a subsistence farmer in a developing nation tills his land to survive whether he is passionate about it or not—but that doesn't dilute its truthfulness for us. Your life's profession should be derived from your deepest passions. This is why the first step in becoming an entrepreneur is to define *passion* and then locate yours.

The modern West has romanticized the word *passion*. The *Merriam-Webster Dictionary* defines it as "a strong feeling of enthusiasm for something or about doing something"; we typically use it to describe only things that we experience positively. We think of passions as those things that excite you or put a twinkle in your eyes or a bounce in your step. We may have a strong emotion about child abuse, but we wouldn't say we are passionate about it. Yet, even while we've romanticized this word, we've also diluted it. We claim to be passionate about dark chocolate and ultimate Frisbee while at the same time declaring ourselves passionate about parenting our children.

I, too, had an incomplete understanding of the word *passion*, until I decided to research its meaning and history. What I discovered surprised me. The English word *passion* derives from the Latin *passio*, which means "suffering." Even one of the predominant Greek precursors for passion is linked with suffering. The word was first popularized in English in the twelfth century to describe Christ's suffering and death on the cross. This is why Mel Gibson's 2004 epic film about Jesus' execution was titled *The Passion of the Christ*. Even the passionflower was so named because its corona resembles the crown of thorns.

This doesn't mean that our passions should make us miserable or lead to our early demise. But it does challenge the candy-coated definitions many of us have come to accept. Our passions involve the things we love, but they are also much more than that. Passions are those things that we love so much we are willing to suffer for them. It's an experience to be coupled with words like *pain*, *preparation*, *readiness*, *submission*, and *loyalty*.

It's important to remember that passion is not suffering for suffering's sake. It's suffering for the sake of something we love. Why does this matter? Because if passion is just what makes you happy, you'll quit doing it when it becomes too tough or too risky, when you're abandoned or mocked. If you don't care about something enough to endure pain, it is probably not worth pursuing.

So what do you love so much that you're willing to do it even if it hurts you? Even if it kills you? This is the foundation of your life's work. This is the heartbeat of your calling. This is the soil from which your start-up grows.

It's one thing to suffer for the sake of suffering, but an entirely different thing to suffer for the sake of a vision. The former makes you a victim while the latter makes you a victor. Entrepreneurs must be willing to discover—and pay a price—to uncover their life's most passionate mission.

Steve Jobs hated the PC. Not just the computer, but the entire way of thinking it represented. He once said, "If, for some reason, we make some big mistake and IBM wins, my personal feeling is that we are going to enter a computer Dark Age for about twenty years."[1] In an interview in 2003, Jobs used words like *wretched* and *anguish* in describing the phone industry. Steve needed problems to fight. He needed something to suffer for. This passion spurred his most brilliant innovations.

Before Veronica and I moved to Bend, I could have started a thousand different businesses. But I had learned that my profession should be derived from my passion. So I started by asking myself what I loved so much I was willing to suffer for it, and determined that I wanted to devote my life to helping people build the businesses and families they love.

When I think about helping people realize their dreams, my chest burns. My thoughts storm. My feet tap unconsciously. Pondering my passion often means losing sleep as I chase my thinking into the night. Or I drift into a daydream when obsessing over images of what could be—images so real that doing anything else seems irresponsible, if not impossible.

Before I could live out my passion as an entrepreneur, however, I decided to draft a personal purpose statement. You should do the same before going any further. Don't worry if it isn't perfect; you can always tweak it later. Just get something down to help direct your thinking. Most entrepreneurs know what their purpose is, but they can't put it into exact words in a concise sentence or two. As a result, their lives and businesses lack clarity and focus.

So here is mine:

I want to help people find their calling, recognize what is truly important, and love their family in ways that grow connection and trust.

The drafting process shouldn't be a quick one. Spend time brainstorming, write it out a few times, come back to it a couple of days later, and then refine it. Make sure to use plain English. It doesn't have to sound smart. If your purpose statement is too complicated, it will feel either unattainable or unrelatable. Here's a good test: if you can't use it in a casual conversation with a friend, then it's probably too complex. Resist the temptation to skip this step or cut corners. Having a clear and motivating purpose statement is critical to this journey. If you falter at the start, you'll probably stumble before you finish.

Onward.

☑ COMPLETE DAY #1

REMEMBER

Passion is the willingness to suffer for something you love.
#LaunchYourDream

ASK

What's the one activity that you can't imagine living without doing?

BELIEVE

I cannot succeed unless I am willing to suffer for what I love.

DO

List five things that you love so much it hurts. Rank them in order of how passionate you are about them.

DAY 2

Calm in the Storm

Estimated Reading Time: 8 Minutes

One-quarter of Americans say they've considered starting a business, but decided not to.[1] That means, if you're reading this in a coffee shop with twenty-five latte-sipping customers, at least six of them fall into this category. In total, eighty million Americans are failing to live their dreams. What a depressing thought.

One of the most common lies you'll hear when you're planning your future is, "Get a job. Play it safe." We've heard this message so many times, it is ingrained in our collective psyche. As our parents and friends and the American educational system echo this message, we come to believe it. We naturally accept that having a job is more secure than working for ourselves.

Of course, starting a business isn't easy. Nothing worthwhile is. The road is perilous, filled with obstacles and the unpredictable. While it may not be as hard as you assume, it will probably be difficult in ways you never imagined. But do not be fooled into thinking that being an entrepreneur is the *more* risky path. Entrepreneurship is difficult, but failing to follow your dreams is worse. Living a meaningless life is harder. Building someone else's dreams only to realize you were expendable is more difficult.

If you assume that getting a job is playing it safe, try this experiment: Repeat that line to a father who just got laid off because his company's CFO made some bad investments. Tell that to a single mom who was fired for not wearing her uniform correctly. Or try giving it to a college student who lost his part-time job at a call center because the company decided to make some cutbacks. They'll tell you that placing your future in someone else's hands is riskier, not safer, than forging your own path.

Being an entrepreneur is like being a storm chaser. The dream you are chasing is a swirling, twirling, brewing beast of risk. It's dangerous and exhilarating to follow a dream, but if you chase it well and wisely, doing so can be quite an adventure. So if you're going to become a storm chaser, here are three steps that will equip you for what is coming.

Wanting the Storm

Among the most common reasons cited for not starting a business are the worry that it won't succeed, financial concerns about giving up a steady income, and fear that it will negatively affect a person's work-life balance.[2] In short, *fear* is the most common reason that potential entrepreneurs decline to make a business move.

The fear that you'll face difficulty if you start a business is legitimate. Difficult days and sleepless nights will come. But the best entrepreneurs learn to see these obstacles as opportunities. They crave the challenges instead of running from them.

Fear is what you should be afraid of. Someone recently told me that fear is a neutral emotion; all that matters is what you do with it. But since fear is stealing so many hopes from so many people, I'm not so sure that fear is any more emotionally neutral than love or hate. Fear is a devious, dastardly deceiver. He whispers lies into our ears, wakes us up from a good night's sleep, and pours concrete over our feet. As I've said before, fear steals more dreams than failure ever will.

Timid would-be entrepreneurs can't let tomorrow's anxieties steal today's dreams. To eradicate your worries, you have to see the problem of a storm as the promise of a better future.

Walking into the Storm

Once you decide you want to be in the storm, you have to step into it. This is difficult because you'll be tempted often to turn back, to race back to safer, calmer waters. You tell yourself that you should get out while you're ahead and try again at a better time.

Unfortunately, there is never an easy time to start a business. No matter how long you wait, you'll never be experienced enough, you'll never have enough capital, and you'll never have zero risk. There's always a chance that your business will fail, but there's also always a chance that it will succeed. As Amazon founder Jeff Bezos has said, "I knew that if I failed I wouldn't regret that, but I knew the one thing I might regret is not trying."[3]

The age-old adage is true, if trite: "Quitters never win and winners never quit." So you have to convince yourself early that quitting isn't an option. Once you stop looking for a way out of the storm, you can focus your energy on finding a way through it.

Weathering the Storm

Many potential starters have idealized prominent entrepreneurs like Walt Disney, John D. Rockefeller, Oprah Winfrey, and Bill

Gates. We imagine them as underdogs who fought their way to success with nothing except ingenuity. But "lone wolf" entrepreneur stories are myths, and most of these entrepreneurs can tell you that they were successful largely because of the teams they surrounded themselves with.

The best start-ups are led by people who are entrenched in community. They are supported by their friends, family, and acquaintances. This isn't by chance, but by design. Those who dare to enter the storm alone are taking a grave and unnecessary risk. Having a community means having people to lift you up when you lose and to celebrate you when you win. It means having a rich well of wisdom from which to draw in confusing and confounding times. It means keeping people close who can remind you of why you've chosen this path.

Many people don't do community well because they don't want to pay what true community costs. We don't want to be responsible for anybody or for anybody to be responsible for us. As individualistic Americans with a spirit of independence, we opt for autonomy. But community is a hard-fought idea that requires giving up a level of autonomy. It's not the sweet, syrupy idea you learned about in Sunday school. Accountability is the glue that ties commitment to results, so it is worthwhile for entrepreneurs. It means making a lasting covenant with a group of people, one that can't be revoked because you're too busy or bored with it. We need each other more than we know. But meeting this need is not free of charge.

Find two or three people who would commit to supporting you on your journey of entrepreneurship. Identify anyone who might hold you back or feel uncomfortable with you doing this, and steer clear. Gather experienced entrepreneurs around you who can help navigate these new and often difficult waters.

If you learn to confront the storm, you'll conquer the storm.

☑ COMPLETE DAY #2

☐  **REMEMBER**

Today isn't rehearsal. This is your life.
#LaunchYourDream

☐  **ASK**

As you start your business, what is the biggest fear you're facing? (Be specific.)

☐ **BELIEVE**

Starting my business is less dangerous than sacrificing my dreams.

☐ **DO**

Ask one person to hold you accountable. Give them permission to ask you about your fears, opportunities, and progress each week.

DAY 3

Personal Preparation

Estimated Reading Time: 10 Minutes

A friend of mine once told me that the recipe for successful entrepreneurship has at least two ingredients: preparation and perspiration. He's right. Becoming a starter means laying the groundwork for the future and working tirelessly to realize that future. But in another sense, those two ingredients are really just one. Preparation *is* perspiration. Paving the road to occupational freedom requires breaking a sweat.

Yesterday, we talked about thinking like an entrepreneur. Launching a successful business is not a matter of putting on a uniform, signing a membership card, or paying your annual union dues. Your mind-set matters. So you have to be in a constant state of learning. Since you've continued on to day three, I assume you learned the importance of learning.

But preparing to be an entrepreneur is more than a matter of the mind. It is also a matter of the eyes, heart, and hands. Some work needs to be done *before* you can do the work you've been called to do. Preparation in the present is paramount to your success in the future. Remember, it wasn't raining when Noah built the ark.

Think back to when you were a kid. One of the most thrilling times in a child's year comes at the close of the summer, when a new school year is about to dawn. We may have been sad to wave good-bye to endless sunshine and late-night bedtimes, but we were equally excited to embrace new adventures and new friendships. As kids, we knew (in part thanks to our parents) that entering a new season should be a time of intense preparation.

As the school year approached, our parents took us to school to locate our classrooms and meet our teachers. They carted us off to the neighborhood mega-mart, where we navigated the family-filled aisles in search of book bags, Trapper Keeper binders, and paper. The night before school began, we cleaned our rooms, set our alarm clocks, and made sure to get enough sleep.

When the day finally arrived, we poured into the new school. We looked around the classroom and realized that every child was one of two kinds of students: prepared or unprepared. Those in the former group had neatly combed hair, found their chairs early, and lined sharpened pencils across the tops of their desks. Students in the latter group rushed into class late, tripping over untied shoelaces, only to realize they were in the wrong homeroom. While most of us are no longer full-time students, the same two categories still apply.

Launching a start-up means beginning a new season. And much like a school year, it requires a time of intense preparation. Approximately 145,000 new businesses start each year in America. About 137,000 of them declare bankruptcy in the first 365 days. I've noticed that most often, those that fail early are those launched by people who skipped the critical work of preparation.

Just like a student, you need to make sure your bag is filled with the right items before the first day of your new season. Here are three tasks that should be on every entrepreneur's prelaunch shopping list.

Identify Your Weaknesses

The ancient Greek adage says, "Know thyself." I would add that you must know *all* of yourself: the good parts and the bad, your strengths and your weaknesses. Most of us are better at knowing half of ourselves. Those of us who grew up with adoring parents or teachers and watched *Mister Rogers' Neighborhood* each afternoon already know that we're "special." We know what we're good at because people have reminded us of it our entire lives—we may even still have the trophies and ribbons to prove it. But we may not be as aware of our flaws.

Before you launch a start-up, you should pause and take a hard look at your weaknesses. We often like looking through windows more than staring into mirrors, but unattended imperfections can often become fatal flaws for entrepreneurs. Are you dishonest or manipulative, easily distracted or obsessive, a poor writer or reckless money manager? There is no need to feel too bad about these flaws. Reasonable explanations for their development may exist. But that doesn't mean they should be ignored. As Steve Maraboli said, "Just because your pain is understandable doesn't mean your behavior is acceptable."[1]

Enlisting trusted friends to help you identify your most dangerous flaws may be a good idea. Give those closest to you permission to tell you the truth about what they see. If you have a booger hanging from your face at an important dinner, a good friend won't keep his mouth shut. He'll pull you aside and let you know that you have a bat falling out of the cave.

Weaknesses in your personal life will often bleed into your professional life. So once you've identified your greatest weaknesses, work to eradicate them from your life. If you don't, they may come back to haunt or hurt you. What you don't know actually can kill you—or at least keep you from being a successful entrepreneur.

Adopt a Rigorous Work Ethic

Close your eyes and envision everything you know about workplace expectations in a giant pile. Now put that pile in an imaginary bag and throw it in an imaginary Dumpster. You're an entrepreneur now. The rules have changed.

You no longer get credit for showing up to work at a certain time. You no longer have the luxury of clocking out at five o'clock and then pretending you didn't see the after-hours e-mails. You no longer get paid for taking extended lunches or long bathroom breaks. When you launch your start-up, your work schedule will likely increase and your wage per hour will probably drop. Start-ups aren't built with financial capital; they are floated down a river of sweat.

In the first stages of launching your business, you may not focus on your venture full-time. Many people initially work another job and devote one to two hours per day to ideation and development. But these hours don't materialize out of thin air. They must come from somewhere. Begin preparing to make cuts in other areas. You may need to give up your Saturday Netflix binge session or the poker night with your college buddies for a while. Ask yourself what you need to give up. An entrepreneur's work ethic always comes with a price tag attached.

Learn to Manage Expectations

Because your schedule is going to change, you need to proactively manage the expectations of those who depend on you for social support. You need to set expectations with your friends and family before you start. Let them know that you are entering a season that may require more of your time. Ask for their support and permission to proceed. It takes a village to launch a start-up.

To be clear, I'm not asking you to become a workaholic. I'm encouraging you to be a smart, structured worker with a flexible schedule. This means building boundaries to keep you from overworking and making sure you don't forget to have fun and invest in those who matter most. Entrepreneurship happens in spurts and seasons. Problems arise when a busy season becomes a string of seasons and you become isolated from those around you.

When you ask your friends for support, also ask them for accountability to help you work hard without being consumed by it. Open a channel of communication that lets them feel comfortable telling you when you're doing too much or losing sight of your true priorities. Build boundaries now, not later. Don't pack your schedule to the brim. Margin is what we need to succeed.

If you were to summarize the three preparation points above with a single word, that word would be *discipline.* I define *discipline* as doing things we don't necessarily like to achieve something we love. It means cutting the fat from your life. It means asking tough questions and taking the time to craft better answers. It means waking up at the same time every day. Because if you can't control your morning, you can't control your day. And if you can't control your day, you can't control your life. Implementing important disciplines during your preparation phase is not the easiest way, but it is the better way.

If you aren't willing to overcome something as small as your schedule, then put this book down and start e-mailing résumés to potential employers. The person who wants to start a business without doing the hard work of preparation will never start a business.

☑ COMPLETE DAY #3

☐ REMEMBER

"Success is where preparation and opportunity meet."

—Bobby Unser

☐ ASK

Think about a time in your life when you failed to prepare for an important event. How would the situation have been better if you had readied yourself?

☐ BELIEVE

If I fail to prepare, I am preparing to fail.

☐ DO

Set up a meeting today with three trusted friends. Ask them to help you identify your most harmful weaknesses.

DAY 4

A Ship That Won't Sail

Estimated Reading Time: 7 Minutes

Of the first seven businesses I launched, six were partnerships. Of those six, each ended less desirably than I would have hoped. Pain, loss, frustrations, unmet expectations, and even legal issues were involved. If my experience was all I had to go on, I would tell every entrepreneur I met to run from partnerships and launch a business on your own.

Luckily, my experience isn't all I have. According to *Forbes*, more than eight out of ten partnerships fail within three years. That's higher than America's divorce rate! That's because when you partner with someone to start a business, you end up spending far too much time together, have more than your share of contentious financial squabbles, and reap far fewer benefits than you would if you had just married the person instead.[1]

Statistically speaking, partnerships don't make running a business easier either. In my experience, you'll end up spending a huge chunk of your workday managing the partnership when you should be building the business. If you were thinking of launching a partnership, I want to take a moment and give you all the reasons you shouldn't. I might just help you avoid the longest, costliest migraine of your life and maybe save a friendship. And if you weren't thinking about launching a partnership, you shouldn't skip this either. If your business gets off the ground, you'll likely be approached by investors or other future partners. My hope is that you'll remember what I'm about to say and run from them as though your shirt were on fire.

Here are four of the most common factors behind why people enter into partnerships and why they fall flat:

1. **Denial:** You *think* you work well with others. You *think* you are great at being a coleader. You *think* a fifty-fifty split works well for both parties. But everyone who knows you best can tell you that you're kidding yourself. And deep down you agree.

   Most entrepreneurs have strong opinions and specific visions about their business. Even introverted starters are A-type leaders and need to establish a system that will let them operate as A-type leaders. When we live in denial of ourselves, we can end up destroying others.
2. **Impatience:** People often take on business partners to speed up the process. It's difficult to deny that two people instead of one means twice the personnel and often twice the financial capital. That's just math.

   The problem is that the equation must be calculated over time. If entrepreneurs will just slow down and conserve money, they will often find they can get to the same place a partnership would take them. And when they arrive there, they have a greater chance of professional success with a lower chance of relational failure. Often the answer is to get creative—hire an intern or call in a favor—rather than give away a piece of the pie.

3. **Guilt:** Sometimes people give away a percentage of ownership or shares of stock to high performers or longtime employees. They'll often claim this act is generosity for others' loyalty and performance, but scratch the surface and you'll find it is often just guilt.

   Rewarding excellence is laudable—remember: this is all coming from a guy who wrote a book titled *People Over Profit*—but you don't have to make poor business decisions to value others. You wouldn't give a landscaper 10 percent of your property if he did a bang-up job trimming your hedges. Don't give away your company because you feel guilty that you aren't doing more to value your employees. Find smarter ways to express your gratitude for their good work.
4. **Insecurity:** Entrepreneurs often bring on partners to help them launch a company because they don't believe they have the business smarts to make it successful. So they partner with someone they think has what they lack. But this ends up being a bad solution to a real problem. If I don't know what a word means, I need to learn the definition, not buy a library of dictionaries. In the same way, taking on a partner is not the best way to educate yourself. A partnership always gives away more than it gains.

Maybe you're thinking of finding a business partner. Perhaps you and a good friend have an idea for a new business. As you prepare to move forward, you need to honestly ask if you believe that you are one of the 20 percent of entrepreneurs who can make a partnership work. Luckily, you don't have to accept those odds.

Being an entrepreneur is like playing an instrument. It's not the number of years you've invested that counts; it's the number of hours. How long you've been doing it matters less than how much you've done it. Invest the hard work necessary to beat back the denial, incompetence, guilt, and insecurity that plagues you. You'll destroy the lie telling you that you're better with a co-captain rather than steering your own vessel. Trust me. The only ship that won't sail is a partnership.

☑ COMPLETE DAY #4

☐ **REMEMBER**

"The only ship that doesn't sail is a partnership."
—Dave Ramsey

☐ **ASK**

Would you enter into a partnership if you believed beyond a shadow of a doubt that you could do it alone—even if it took a little longer? If so, what's keeping you from going it alone?

☐ **BELIEVE**

It's possible and not prideful to launch my business without a partner.

☐ **DO**

List three reasons you *wouldn't* make a good business partner.

Dream Well

DAY 5

An Irresistible Idea

Estimated Reading Time: 10 Minutes

Entrepreneurs are more than just a growing part of the American economy. They are now a significant part of American folklore. We often hear stories about Steve Jobs at Apple or Mark Zuckerberg at Facebook and assume that a critical part of being a successful entrepreneur is youthfulness. But according to recent research, the average age of a successful entrepreneur in high-growth industries such as aerospace and health care is forty. Twice as many successful entrepreneurs are over the age of fifty as compared to those under the age of twenty-five.[1] The determining factor in a starter's success isn't age; it often depends on the strength of their ideas.

If you've picked up this book and read this far, you probably have an idea for a service or product that you believe has marketplace value. I hate to be the bearer of bad news, but your idea may suck. Lots of entrepreneurs have bad ideas. But the best ones will continue to search until they replace a bad idea with a good one or find a better version of the bad idea.

But that raises a question: how does an entrepreneur know

if an idea is good or bad? Some assume that the value of an idea is in the eye of the beholder, and when it comes to the details of your idea, that may be true. If an entrepreneur came to me with a new type of soda, I wouldn't be interested. I don't like soda, and I don't drink it. But just because I don't consider it a good idea *for me* doesn't mean it is inherently bad.

The true value of an idea, however, is not a matter of taste. This is actually one of the worst ways to judge an idea's merits. The reason for this is "confirmation bias," or the human tendency to filter facts according to what we hope is true. As Richard Watson of *Fast Company* wrote, "If someone has an idea that they believe in, then any fact that supports the idea will be quickly seized upon, whereas any fact that questions it will be instantly dismissed."[2]

Entrepreneurs need objective measures by which to judge their business ideas. In my experience, the best ideas have four characteristics that enable success, like the four legs that support a stool.

They Solve a Problem

Often, entrepreneurs create a product that is a solution in search of a problem. The best start-ups, however, are built on problem solving. As bestselling author Seth Godin says, "Don't find customers for your products, find products for your customers." As long as consumers have problems, they will always search for solutions and you will always have a business. Your ideas are only as strong as the problems they solve.

Of course, problems are like people. There are big ones and tiny ones, quiet ones and noisy ones. How do you know if your idea seeks to solve a worthy one? The best problems to solve are built around three elements:

1. Necessity: Search for problems that people *need* to solve. That will make your good or service a "must-have," not a "nice-to-have." Ideas that solve deep-seated issues have more potential than luxury products that tackle fringe problems.
2. Pain: The more pain the problem causes, the more powerful the solution will be. If your idea can relieve significant pain in the life of your customer, you'll find quick buy-in and create lifelong fans. If a problem causes physical, emotional, even financial pain, it is a good one to solve.
3. Urgency: If there is a time component involved, the power of your idea can be amplified. A new kind of chemotherapy that can cure a lethal form of cancer is a more lucrative product than a new form of ibuprofen that is more sensitive on the stomach. The latter isn't nearly as urgent as the former.

They Scratch Your Own Itch

This leg of the stool is related to the last point. You need to make sure that both the idea—and the problem it seeks to solve—are important to you personally. Working to solve someone else's problem is never the best choice. Don't start a baby clothing company if you don't have children. Don't start a tour guide service for mountain climbers if you're afraid of heights. You have a better outlook and a greater chance of success if you align your personal interests and life with your business ideas.

As Brian Hamilton, chairman of Sageworks, said:

There are entrepreneurs who can start businesses in industries they don't care about—buy for a dollar, sell for two. These

> *people exist; I just haven't seen any successful ones. On average, I think you'll find that most successful business owners were (and are) passionate about the original idea behind their companies. The best entrepreneurs are like a musician who has a song and must sing it.*[3]

Likewise, make sure the idea fits with your lifestyle. If you can't afford it, it's probably not your idea. And if you don't enjoy it, it probably isn't your idea. Filmmaking icon Walt Disney may have said it best: "We don't make movies to make money. We make money to make more movies."

They Are Timed Right

At least one person had a vision for Netflix, a company that has helped dismantle the cable industry in America. At least one person had a vision for Airbnb, a company that has rocked the traditional hotel industry in America. At least one person had a vision for Uber, a company that has sent the public transportation industry in America scrambling. The ideas behind all three corporations have been wildly lucrative and have spawned a cottage industry of knockoffs. But one important thing they all have in common is timing.

A great idea launched at an inopportune time is a bad idea. Imagine if you had an idea for a revolutionary brick-and-mortar travel agency or a new and improved pay-phone booth. In the early 1990s these may have been good ideas, but today anyone will tell you that they are bad ideas. The only thing that's different is the timing.

Timing is about more than just time. It's not just when your idea occurs, but what is happening in the world, in your industry, and in the marketplace. Brandon Watts, a renowned publicist who has represented scores of start-ups, said:

> [Good] timing isn't about launching in either this or that quarter. Rather, it's about the much broader condition of the industry and culture as a whole—something that can't usually be controlled by business leaders and in many ways can't even be defined. For entrepreneurs, it can be hard to accept that something so mysterious can make or break their companies, especially when there are so many other factors already working against a startup's success. Yet it's the reality all of them face.[4]

They Are Scalable

A bad idea is one that allows you to make money only if you have more time, so it is wholly dependent on you. Why? Because that kind of idea has a ceiling. Even the hardest-working entrepreneurs ultimately run out of time. And when they do, they'll grow frustrated and burned-out trying to grow their business when growth is no longer possible. The best idea is one that can be scaled so that the entrepreneur can make more money while investing less time.

In the end, putting your energy behind the best idea possible only increases your chance of success. It doesn't guarantee success. You'll also need to be a passionate entrepreneur with a killer work ethic and a boatload of patience. An idea can be good, but only you can make it irresistible.

☑ COMPLETE DAY #5

☐ **REMEMBER**

"The value of an idea lies in the using of it."

—Thomas A. Edison

☐  **ASK**

If you stated the problem you're trying to solve in one sentence, what would that be?

☐ **BELIEVE**

My ideas are only as strong as the problems they solve.

☐ **DO**

Rate how your idea measures on each of the following criteria, on a scale of 1 to 5:

The problem I'm solving is a necessity. ___

The problem I'm solving is painful. ___

The problem I'm solving is urgent. ___

The problem I'm solving is timely. ___

The problem I'm solving is scalable. ___

The problem I'm solving fits my lifestyle. ___

DAY 6

A Three-Part Foundation

Estimated Reading Time: 10 Minutes

One of the most famous comic strips by the legendary *Peanuts* illustrator, Charles Schulz, depicts Linus sitting in a pile of sand. He plunges his hands into the grains to shape them into an elaborate castle with doors, windows, and flag-topped turrets. The sculpture is masterful. But then Linus looks up and sees the rain begin to fall. The skies open and water pours out. In the final scene Linus is sitting in the middle of a wet, flat stretch of mud where his sand castle once proudly stood. He says, "There's a lesson to be learned here somewhere, but I don't know what it is."

The irony was not lost on Schulz's readers who were raised in the Christian tradition. In the gospel of Matthew, Jesus tells a parable of two men who build two houses. One builds his house on rock and the other on sand. But when the rain falls and the floodwaters rise, the beachfront property washes away while the rock-anchored house remains. What is the moral of Jesus' story? Success often depends on the foundation.

What is true for building a house is true for building a start-up. Too many entrepreneurs rush to buy siding and shutters for their new construction without first creating a strong foundation that will last. This seems to work for a while—and then the first flood comes. A lawsuit is filed or a key employee resigns or a top leader has a moral failing. Without a solid foundation, the business they've built begins to disintegrate.

Tomorrow, we will talk about your business plan. But before we can hang those shutters, we need to pour some concrete and construct a frame. There are three components to the foundation of every business that a leader cannot afford to bypass.

Mission

The mission is the soul of your business. It shapes all you do as a company. It should capture the essence of what you're working toward as an organization. As Dave Ramsey wrote, "Without a really good mission statement you have the potential to get to the top of the ladder only to find it is leaning against the wrong building."[1] Without a clear mission statement, your start-up will never rise to the level of its potential. A company with money is no match against a company on a mission.

When I help entrepreneurs craft mission statements for their organizations, I encourage them to opt for concrete language over vague wording and tell them to make it feel big and bold. I also believe it is best to limit the mission to a single sentence and to begin with the word *to*. Disney's mission statement is "To make people happy," and Amazon's mission statement is "To be the world's most customer-centric company."

An easy way for starters to think of their mission statement is as an extension of their personal purpose statement. Since your purpose statement springs from your passion, linking the two statements ensures that the mission of your business will be an outgrowth of your personal passion.

My personal purpose statement is "To help people find their calling, recognize what is truly important, and love their family in ways that grow connection and trust." The mission statement for StartupCamp is "To help people turn their passion into a profession that improves their freedom, family, and finances." See the connection?

Vision

Having clear, addictive, and motivating vision is crucial to your venture. Although many business leaders fail to differentiate between their mission and vision, the two are separate and distinct. A vision statement has more color, can be longer, and looks to an achievable goal from five to ten years ahead. It's broader than merely wishing for something, and it's deeper than simply wanting more. It is the ability to envision a desirable future with such clarity that you can see plainly the steps you must take to get there.

It needs to be attainable, but just barely. Think of a vision statement as an idea that is almost unrealistic. Your ability to transfer this vision to others will become the currency of your growth. It's your magic wand in getting people to join your journey. It includes both the *what* and the *who* of your vision.

My friend Scott Harrison runs a company called Charity:Water that has galvanized a global movement to provide access to clean drinking water in areas where people lack it. His organization's vision statement is "To provide clean and safe drinking water to every person on the planet." Sounds pretty bold, huh? I'd call it barely attainable. Charity:Water is now moving swiftly toward its goal at a rate of 2,700 people per day.

The vision statement of StartupCamp is "To help one million people start their own business, spend time with their families, and experience the adventure of entrepreneurship." We've helped thousands through our online curriculum, and the book you're holding will help thousands more. I'm hoping to surpass the goal of our vision statement within five to ten years of our founding.

Values

Entrepreneur magazine calls values "the North Star guide to your startup."[2] These are the timeless principles you are committed to as an organization. These are hills on which you are prepared to die. No compromising, no capitulating. At the e-commerce company I founded, one of the values was "people matter." When we fired someone, for example, we let them go the way we would want to be let go. We even threw them a party, to affirm their best attributes and qualities. We thought of past employees as alumni who had graduated to jobs more aligned with their gifts.

Lots of business leaders today talk about core values, but many do a poor job of incorporating them. It's nice to frame your values and hang them on the wall of your office. But that wooden rectangle is meaningless if it doesn't change the way your company operates. Also, if you have fifteen core values, then you need to start over. If you call them "core," then you shouldn't have more than five. These values need to be simple and are more for your team than for your customers. Here are three values we seek to honor at StartupCamp:

1. **Design:** We believe design is more important than most people assume. Our meticulous and thoughtful aesthetics subtly communicate that we care about details. If you know we care about details, then you know we care about customers.
2. **Family:** Money isn't everything, and neither is growth. Your family is paramount. Because of this value, our employees can challenge us if we ask them to all work fifty-five hours per week. At StartupCamp, we emphasize that the nine to five is not more important than the five to nine.
3. **Brilliance:** We value the question "Why?" (More on this later.) Our team never makes decisions based on intuition *or* information—always both. If people feel we should do something, we will always ask them why.

Do not postpone drafting your values until after launching. Your values will help you know right from wrong as opposed to knowing just legal from illegal. Something may be legal, but it could still be wrong for you and your company. Your values shape how your people act, react, and live inside your business.

Being an entrepreneur means jumping from rainstorm to rainstorm. If you're not experiencing a flood now, you've probably just come out of one. If neither, brace yourself, because you're about to walk into one. By fortifying a three-part foundation *before* you start, not *after*, you'll always be ready for the rain.

☑ COMPLETE DAY #6

☐ REMEMBER

If you don't know who you are, you'll never know what you are.
#LaunchYourDream

☐ ASK

What is one change you can make today to better incorporate your mission, vision, and values into your daily operations?

☐ BELIEVE

My direction, not my intention, determines my start-up's destination.

☐ DO

Draft your mission statement, vision statement, and three core values.

DAY 7

A Business Doesn't Happen by Accident

Estimated Reading Time: 11 Minutes

One of the most frequent comments I receive from readers who've followed my life is, "Dale, you're so lucky." They look at pictures of my farm and family on Instagram, they witness my business successes, they read one of my books, and they can't believe I have achieved it all by my early thirties. If by *lucky* they mean blessed by God, then I can accept that what they are saying is at least partially true. But often we talk about luck to avoid acknowledging someone's planning and hard work, and by extension, to avoid acknowledging our own lack of planning and hard work.

I remember, as a kid, my dad leaving the house to work for nearly twelve hours per day. He would wake up before the sun did and leave around five thirty each morning, if not earlier. In the afternoons, the door would swing open at almost four o'clock and my dad would walk inside exhausted. I've always been grateful for my dad's willingness to make these sacrifices for his family. Witnessing his work ethic has made me more determined in my own life. But I also decided early in life to live a different life, and I began to make plans accordingly. Today I work from home, where I can eat lunch with my wife and play with my kids on breaks. I get to enjoy the freedom of being my own boss and planning my own schedule. This isn't luck; it was planned.

As young adults, my parents struggled under the weight of car payments and credit card balances. Later in life, they worked hard to become debt-free. This was an inspiration to me, and I decided not to live as a slave to debt. I planned early to live below my means and to avoid debt whenever possible. Today, I enjoy financial freedom. I'm not lucky or merely blessed; I planned for this.

I remember thinking in my twenties, *I don't want to be an old grandfather.* I wanted to enjoy my family as early as possible. So I began to pray for and look for a wife. After I married Veronica, we quickly began to talk about starting a family so that children were not something that just happened to us. I bought a farm in Oregon because I wanted our family to live sustainably and because I wanted my kids to have a connection to the land. I guess you could say I live a lucky life, but I'd also tell you we planned for this.

People who fail to plan end up with a less-than-desirable life and wonder why. But the lack of planning *is* the reason why. Pastor Andy Stanley often tells ministry leaders, "Your current template is perfectly designed to produce the results you are currently getting." This is true not just for ministries and for families but also for start-ups. If you want to launch a successful business, you need a succinct business plan.

So you've formulated your business idea. And you've vetted it to make sure it is sound. What now? You need to translate all those great ideas into words. You need to form your idea into a plan. The business plan is one of the greatest learning experiences an entrepreneur can have. Contrary to popular belief, the business plan is not for investors, or partners, or banks. It's for *you*, so you can fully understand who you are, the viability of your idea, and the strategies you will use to turn your dream into a profitable reality. As Jeff Haden, contributing editor of *Inc.* magazine, wrote:

> Some entrepreneurs succeed without a business plan. With great timing, solid business skills, entrepreneurial drive, and a little luck, some founders build thriving businesses without ever creating even an informal business plan.
>
> But the chances are more likely that those entrepreneurs fail.
>
> Will a business plan make success inevitable? Absolutely not. But great planning often means the difference between success and failure.[1]

You don't have to take my word for it, or Haden's. Clemson University entrepreneurship professor William B. Gartner was once skeptical about the importance of writing a business plan. So he decided to study it. He and his colleagues surveyed data from the Panel Study of Entrepreneurial Dynamics, a national survey of more than eight hundred starters. What they found shocked many in the business world.

According to Gartner, writing a business plan is not necessarily correlated with whether a company will be successful. It's not a silver bullet. However, entrepreneurs who write a plan are two and a half times more likely to follow through and launch their businesses.[2] Taking the time to draw up a business plan transforms your talk into walk.

Below is my twelve-point structure for writing your business plan. It has three sections with four points each. It has served me well over the past decade, and it will work for you no matter what kind of start-up you're planning to launch.

Section One: Company Overview

1. What Does Your Business Do?
    a. Describe your business in one to two sentences.
    b. Describe your business in one to two paragraphs.
    c. What makes your business unique?
2. Who Are You?
    a. What is your company's mission, vision, and core values?
3. Customer Pain
    a. What is your customer's problem, and how is your organization solving it?
4. Organizational Chart
    a. Who is currently on staff?
    b. What positions do you expect to fill in the near future?
    c. What current positions are sitting empty?

Section Two: Product and Operational Strategies

1. Product Overview
    a. What do you make or provide?
    b. What makes it better, stronger, and different?
    c. If you're making a product, where will you source or manufacture it?
    d. If applicable, describe your packaging and shipping.
    e. Is any technology required to process payments or sell your product?

2. Customer Overview
    a. Who is your customer?
    b. How old are they?
    c. Where do they live?
    d. What are your customer's beliefs, hobbies, fears, and passions?
    e. What do market trends tell you about your customer?
    f. Who is not your customer?
3. Marketing Overview
    a. How will people learn about your start-up?
    b. What metrics will help you evaluate your progress?
    c. What two to three social media channels will become your main line of communication?
    d. What influencers could you realistically partner with to bring more awareness to what you're doing?
    e. Where will you spend advertising money, and how much?
4. SWOT Analysis (**S**trengths, **W**eaknesses, **O**pportunities, **T**hreats)
    a. List five to ten of your company's greatest strengths.
    b. List five to ten of your company's weaknesses.
    c. List five to ten marketplace opportunities available to your customer.
    d. List five to ten of your company's greatest threats.

Section Three: Financial Projections and Capital Needs

1. Financial Projections
    a. How much revenue will your start-up make in 1, 3, 6, and 12 months after launch?

   b. What will be your expenses by 1, 3, 6, and 12 months after launch?
   c. What is your monthly margin (the percentage difference between costs and expenses)?
   d. How much net profit will be made in this 1-, 3-, 6-, and 12-month span?
2. Competitive Environment
   a. List at least three potential competitors, along with their strengths and weaknesses.
   b. What three things can you copy from your competitors to make your business stronger?
3. Capital Needs
   a. How much money do you need to launch and sustain your business for the first year?
   b. How will you generate income during your first year in business? (Possibly it will be your current day job.)
4. Use of Funds Schedule
   a. How will you spend your money each month? (Document every dollar.)

Over the last twelve years, I've written and executed eleven comprehensive business plans, and they have enabled me to raise over $2.5 million. (Our full curriculum gives a comprehensive example of a business plan, and you can download a copy of the one I wrote for StartupCamp at StartupCamp.com/businessplan.) By *comprehensive*, I do not mean it must be long. My typical business plan is about five to ten pages, and yours will probably be on the low end of that scale. Set aside ninety minutes or so to create the first draft of your plan. Block out interruptions, and if possible do it with someone you trust rather than alone.

If you have a business idea but don't know where to start,

you need to draft a plan. If you have a start-up that's progressing slowly, you need to draft a plan. If you require venture capital to take your company to the next level, you need to draft a plan. The most reliable way to predict the future is to plan it.

☑ COMPLETE DAY #7

☐ REMEMBER

"He who fails to plan is planning to fail."

—Winston Churchill

ASK

Which section of the business plan do you think will be most difficult for you to follow, and why?

☐ BELIEVE

Without a plan, my start-up is just a dream.

DO

Using the template provided in this chapter, write your five-page business plan in ninety minutes.

Make ’Em Feel It

DAY 8

Whyology

Estimated Reading Time: 9 Minutes

Every piece of marketing and brand strategy you produce as an entrepreneur will stem from how you answer a one-word question: Why? I encountered this idea a few years ago in a TED Talk by Simon Sinek, "How Great Leaders Inspire Action," which sent me on a worldview-shifting journey. In his talk, Sinek popularized the now famous idea that "people don't buy *what* you do; they buy *why* you do it." The more I researched this idea as it related to start-ups, the more it rang true. Since then, lots of writers and researchers like me have begun to build upon this idea and change the way starters understand business.

As I talk to entrepreneurs across the country, I am realizing how few heed this "why wisdom." Most business leaders know *what* products they sell and *what* services they provide. Some may even know *how* they do business differently from their competitors. But very few starters have taken the time to define *why* they do what they do.

Your company's why is your purpose. It's your calling. It's the bridge between your personal and professional beliefs. Defining your why can be difficult, but failing to do it often turns out to be a fatal mistake.

The "whyology" of business is as simple as arithmetic, but it is rooted in science. An entrepreneur's why is driven from deep inside his or her brain's limbic system—the portion of your gray matter that is responsible for emotions, trust, loyalty, and gut-level decisions. This portion of the brain has no capacity for language. It's a silent chunk of feelings. It lacks the capacity to put those feelings into words.

If I ask someone why he loves his wife, he might spew out a list of facts and features: her strength, her thoughtfulness, her tenderness, and so on. But this doesn't get to the core. If I kept pressing him to answer my question, he may lash out in frustration: "Because—I just do!" Humans' inability to produce emotional answers is quite common. It's difficult for us to withdraw words from the emotional bank in our brains.

On the contrary, the neocortex portion of the brain is responsible for facts, figures, analyzing, and data. It's also where we house all of our capacity for language. This lump of gray matter is the part of us that asks the limbic brain the incredibly important question "Should I care?" The most common reply we receive is no.

Because this is also the way consumer psychology functions, it explains why most marketing fails. Most advertisers begin by describing what their brand does with a long list of facts and figures—the what. An automobile advertisement might say, "The new model of our car goes 0 to 60 in 5.5 seconds." They are appealing to the neocortex. When they follow up by asking consumers if they want to click, read more, watch, or purchase, the neocortex asks the limbic brain if it cares, and when it hears nothing, it moves on.

The best marketing for your start-up will not attempt to

hook consumers primarily with the *what* or even the *how*, but the *why*. It will appeal to the limbic brain before the neocortex. This makes sense for reasons that transcend human biology.

Think about it. If you center on the what, then you're competing with the noise created by thousands of pitches and ploys that consumers have learned to filter out of their minds. You become one what in a sea of whats, and your chance of success plummets. If you center on the how, then you'll be one lone starter forced to compete against giant corporations whose hows are more sophisticated and proven than yours. You'll likely fail. But no one else has your why, so if you lead with that, you'll become a unique solution that is connecting with the consumer's emotional core.

Suppose I wanted to place an advertisement for StartupCamp.com's online course on social media. I can choose to lead with one of three components:

- **What =** Provide education for aspiring entrepreneurs.
- **How =** A twelve-month course supported by a committed community, constant resources, and consistent accountability.
- **Why =** Dreams are worth chasing.

If I took the most common approach, I would design some slick banner ads and overlay the following text: "StartupCamp.com has over 1,000 members, includes hundreds of educational articles, and offers an easy guide to launching a business. Do you want to sign up?" Would that ad compel you to click and spend money? Maybe, but likely not.

A better message for StartupCamp.com might lead instead with the why: "We believe dreams are worth chasing. It's our hope to provide a transformational coaching program to help people start their own business and create the life they love. Are you ready to chase your dream?"

This message is better received by your brain, right? The reason is that I opened up by speaking to your limbic brain and centering on my company's unique message. My emotional statement skipped your neocortex altogether, and then I fed you the facts and figures second. This is how the best start-ups position their brand.

The secret is in the first sentence—what I call the whyology statement—that every company needs. This statement usually becomes your tagline and should be one of the first things people notice when they land on your website, see your business card, or encounter marketing collateral. A simple tip to writing it is to begin with the phrase "I believe" or "we believe." It should be short—a few words, maybe five max. I once launched a successful website that sold sporting goods. The whyology statement was "sports connect people."

The stronger your sense of why is, the stronger your start-up will be. As entrepreneur Brian Hamilton said:

> *The "why" behind your business idea is absolutely crucial. It's important to have a vision for your company—a strong internal driver of why it is important for you to be successful. A sense of purpose will help carry you through the unavoidable periods of trial, doubt, and struggle. It helps if, as previously mentioned, you care about what you're doing. When the inevitable tough times come, the ones who hang onto the tree are the ones who are passionate about what they're providing to the marketplace. Otherwise, they will not have the gas to make it through inevitable travails.*[1]

What do you plan to sell or do? What will your start-up do

differently than others? And most important, why do you do what you do?

The whyology statement for my last e-commerce business was "people matter." At one point, we did some A-B market testing to see if that resonated with our customers. We asked one group of people to sign up for alerts, and in exchange we gave them 50 percent off their purchase. Then we asked a second group of people to sign up for alerts using the following marketing copy: "We believe people matter. Every product you buy supports a charity in need." The second message got an exponentially higher response than the first.

Why? Exactly.

☑ COMPLETE DAY #8

☐  **REMEMBER**

"People don't buy what you do, they buy why you do it."
—Simon Sinek

☐ **ASK**

What are five of your customers' most compelling emotional triggers?

☐ **BELIEVE**

If I can't identify my whyology, then I'll never fully connect with my customers.

☐ **DO**

Draft three possible whyology statements for your company. The statement should be no more than five words, not including the preceding phrase "we believe."

DAY 9

Brand School

Estimated Reading Time: 13 Minutes

The branding campaign for the London Olympics in 2012 cost $625,000. It sounds like a lot, but then again, it's all relative. When the British Broadcasting Corporation decided to rebrand, it paid a whopping $1.8 million. When Andersen Consulting relaunched under the name Accenture, the transition cost the firm $100 million. When British Petroleum decided to rebrand in mid-2000, it coughed up $211 million.[1]

For entrepreneurs who have to count their pennies, these figures can sound excessive, even wasteful. But there's a reason huge corporations spend so much money on branding. It's not just to look sexier or appear cooler. It's because they know that like it or not, every company has a brand, and the quality of its brand will determine whether the company sinks or soars.

As business writer Tom Peters famously said in the late 1990s, "The brand is a promise of the value you'll receive."[2] This is even truer today than it was then. A brand for a company is the equivalent of the personality or character or reputation of a person. What's more, a corporate personality is often like a human personality—while the world around it changes, it often stays the same.

Contrary to popular belief, a brand is not a logo. A brand is not a graphic design. A brand is not a product. These should all be an extension of the brand, but they are not the brand itself. No, your brand is the all-encompassing global experience someone has with your organization. It includes your character, your reputation, and the feelings people experience when they hear your name.

If you haven't shaken off the cynicism of the 1990s or harbor a disdain for marketing, you might tell people that you don't have a brand. That you are just who you are. But don't kid yourself. Every business in the digital age has a brand, no exceptions. You have a brand even if you haven't branded yourself. But here is the good news for you: once you accept the reality of the marketplace, you can help shape how your brand is received by your customers. And this point is critical because, as the old saying goes, perception is reality. Your brand is not what you say it is; your brand is what your customers (or potential customers) say it is.

If this topic is beginning to feel overwhelming to you, good. You're starting to grasp its importance. If you're starting to feel confused, good. You're realizing that branding is more complex than most entrepreneurs assume. If you're starting to feel excited, that's also good. Because you're realizing that although challenging, the act of branding is one of the most important steps in launching a business.

Brands and branding are complex creatures, but here are three simple components to help you clear a path.

Create a Strong Personality

It takes a lot to create a consistent corporate personality. Lots of energy. Lots of innovation. Lots of brainpower. Lots of discipline. But because you've defined your mission, vision, values, and whyology statement, you are well ahead of the pack. The organization's brand must reflect its mission, its values must be in sync with how the organization behaves in the marketplace, the design must accurately depict the corporate attitude, customer support should uphold the company's promise—you get the picture.

Lay out your mission, vision, values, and whyology statement. Think about the implications of these elements for your corporate personality. Then write down ten to twenty words that describe your start-up's personality, and think about how these should influence your daily operations. Is your organization friendly or formal, creative or professional, generous or conservative, bright or dark, aggressive or tender? This list will help you know what your brand *feels* like before you consider what your brand should *look* like.

Craft a Fitting Name and Logo

If you've ever left your house during daylight hours, you know the importance of a first impression. What someone thinks when they first see you forms opinions about you that are difficult to undo. When it comes to organizations, the name is often the first impression.

Years ago, I read a book by Marty Neumeier titled *The Brand Gap* that outlined several criteria for a good business name. Reading it got me thinking that the value of a name is more than whether a particular person likes it or not. There are some objective standards of measurements too. Here are four criteria that I think make a good business name:

1. **Likability:** Your name should be fun for people to use and say. Apple is more likable than Innovative Computer

Solutions of Cupertino. You could probably find a more descriptive name for caramel-colored and caffeinated phosphoric acid, but Coca-Cola rolls off your tongue pretty easily. Likable names are better than boring ones.

2. **Brevity:** There once was a company called Southern Ohio Amalgamated Steam Traction Engine and Boiler Manufacturing Company. You'll be shocked to learn that it went out of business in 1924. In general, shorter is better than longer. If I can't remember your name, I won't remember your products.
3. **Simplicity:** This characteristic is connected to the last. Make sure that the name is simple, not overly confusing. A good test for this is to speak the name to someone who has never heard it and see if they can spell it. If your name confuses people, you have created an unnecessary hurdle that customers must jump over in order to fall in love with your start-up. Your name shouldn't turn into a spelling bee.
4. **Protectability:** Finding a name is tricky these days because, among other reasons, almost everything is trademarked. Make sure that your name isn't going to earn you a lawsuit or create confusion when someone types it into a search engine. If someone Googles the name of your cleaning supply company and lands on a pool chemical distributor, you might as well close up your pine-scented shop and go home.

What's in a name? Well, a lot, as it turns out. And because a name is important, so is your logo. If you're not a design expert, please don't handle this part of the branding process yourself. I'm sure your MS Paint skills are unrivaled, but it's worth making sure this is done right.

As you begin to go through the logo design process with a professional, make sure to avoid the common mistake of trying to cram everything about you into it. If you're a fair trade coffee company that sources from farms in Ecuador, that's great. But you don't need a coffee plant budding into a steaming ceramic mug with three farmers' faces on it, all encircled by an outline of the continent of South America. It's just not necessary. As a friend of mine says, "A wealth of information creates a poverty of attention."

Imagine you're attending a party. Suppose two people walk in, and they have their height, weight, and blood type tattooed on their faces. Below their beautiful mugs, they're each wearing a T-shirt that tells you their political party and lists their food allergies. Now imagine you happen to let these weirdos near you, and they hand you a copy of their family tree and tell you their favorite color. Would you be put off? I would. Not because these facts aren't important but because I just don't need them all up front. I like to get to know someone before they rattle off the most intimate details of who they are. Why should you steward your corporate personality any differently?

Dress It All Up

Since a corporate personality is similar to a human one, it doesn't change often. But the elements around your personality change all the time. Your graphic design and website are visual extensions of an internal personality. Think of them like clothes. They can change over time, but they shouldn't be disconnected from who you are on the inside.

If you go to my website, the colors, fonts, and dimensions I've chosen are all intentional. I thought long and hard about whether I wanted a flat design or shadows. Even the words

I choose and the tone I speak in are related to the words that describe my corporate personality. It would be weird to meet a person dressed like a Wyoming wrangler who talked like a member of the British Parliament. So I carefully craft everything.

While these elements are all an extension of your start-up, and therefore an extension of you, some rules do apply. Humans love order, for example, and certain colors complement one another while others clash. So make sure that this process is guided by someone who knows what they are doing.

As you survey these three elements of your brand, you may notice that the goal of branding can be summed up in one word: distinctiveness. Why is there a car service application called Uber? It doesn't say anything about the company, but it is simple, likable, protectable, and brief. And because of this, it stands out. A more descriptive name might be John's Taxi Service, but that dreadful label would have led the company to bankruptcy. When it comes to branding with names and logos, distinctive is better than descriptive.

The best branding will help your start-up stand out among all your competitors. The human mind notices only what's different. If you brand your organization well, you'll be a bright orange dot in a sea of gray ones.

Branding is so important that once you get it right, you need to protect it fiercely. If you need to hire a "brand keeper" to help judge whether design and marketing materials are consistent with your brand, do it. Also, a brand guide is an indispensable tool. This is a list of the organization's guidelines on how the brand should be represented inside and outside of the company. The guide should be around five pages or so and provide specific guidelines on color, fonts, layout, and use of photography. This information is critical to keep your brand consistent, persistent, and restrained. (To download a copy of StartupCamp's brand guide, visit StartupCamp.com/brand-guide.)

Why do companies pay millions of dollars to rebrand themselves? Because branding matters. This would be a perfect time to give you an example of a company that ignored this rule at its peril. But why waste your time? You've never heard of them.

☑ COMPLETE DAY #9

☐ REMEMBER

"Your brand isn't what you say it is, it's what they say it is."

—Marty Neumeier

☐  ASK

What is the number one thing that makes your company different? Write it in one sentence.

☐ BELIEVE

I should focus more on being distinctive than being descriptive.

☐ DO

Developing your brand is not a great place to cut corners. Contact three professional designers to get a quote to help you shape the visual elements of your start-up.

Win Their Hearts

DAY 10

Platform Thinking

Estimated Reading Time: 10 Minutes

In 1989, actor Kevin Costner starred in one of the greatest American films of the modern era. *Field of Dreams* is a fantasy drama about an Iowa farmer who has a troubled relationship with his baseball-loving father. While walking through a cornfield one night, he hears a mysterious voice whisper, "If you build it, he will come." Costner's character replaces part of his cornfield with a baseball field, and long-deceased players begin appearing to play baseball. The baseball diamond becomes a catalyst for life change and community transformation. It's a remarkable story.

But over time, some entrepreneurs have adopted the whispered phrase from that movie as a business principle: if you build it, *they* will come. These starters believe that if they build it—a product, a business, a website—then people will be drawn to it like magnets. *If I build a business,* they believe, *my audience will come.* Unfortunately, this way of thinking is as unrealistic as Costner's movie. Building a start-up is not a magic trick.

In the modern marketplace, you need to find a team before you construct the baseball diamond. Too many people still operate in a mind-set left over from the days when starting a business often meant purchasing a storefront. Fifty years ago, if you wanted to launch an insurance agency or accounting firm or clothing store or pharmacy, you would find a piece of property on Main Street. You'd put your product in the window, hang a sign over the door, and then wait for customers who naturally walked by to stop in and purchase goods as needed. But Main Street has been replaced by the Internet, and most starters in the digital age cannot get by on an outdated *Field of Dreams* way of thinking. Today, you have to build an audience *before* you build a business.

Nothing is worse than watching an entrepreneur launch a business and then realize that nobody is listening. Once these starters realize they launched in the wrong order, they have to pay to play: they have to buy an audience through advertising, which is expensive. Instead, starters should build a base of followers first. Online, this might mean five to ten thousand followers across social media. For a local business, this might mean a thousand people on an e-mail list from across the city.

Building an audience may sound daunting because it is probably novel for you. You've never built a business *and* you've never built an audience. So it may feel as though I've just added another item to your already-full plate. Lucky for you, building an audience is not as difficult as it sounds, and it can usually be done in less time than you probably assumed.

So how do you build an audience in the modern marketplace? The answer can be summarized in three words: content, content, content.

If you want to launch a coffee company, don't expect to put your bags on an online store and become an instant millionaire. It won't happen. I don't care if you have the most efficient supply chain since the advent of Starbucks and the best-tasting dark roast north of the equator. If you don't have an established audience who can purchase your product and tell their friends and family, you've got a steep climb ahead of you. You need to establish a beautiful web presence with a great whyology statement: "We believe coffee is an art." On that site you should be posting well-written articles on coffee culture, interviews with coffee innovators, and recipes for craft coffee drinks. You should start a podcast and a helpful weekly newsletter. And you should be sharing those on social media regularly.

At StartupCamp.com, we release new resources for our audience every week—from articles and podcasts to videos and e-books. We also provide consistent social media posts across most networks that educate, elevate, and entertain our audience when they are not purchasing something from us.

All of our content is connected to our whyology. We're not posting crafty ideas on how to build gingerbread houses or tips for decorating sugar cookies. That's not what we do. Instead, you'll find articles such as "How I Gained over 1 Million Followers on Social Media," "Five Difficult Steps to Becoming a Millionaire," and "How to Blog Yourself to a Realistic Salary."

From these titles, you may already be picking up on what kind of content works best: useful content. Nearly every soul on planet Earth has a working mouth and the ability to write. But your words are only as influential as the power they impart to those who read them. A great influencer understands that he or she must produce content that is bursting with value and meaning. Words that grow people. Words that provide help and hope. Lessons that are of such worth that people are shocked you've given them away at no cost.

What is the content strategy for your company? Surprisingly, most starters—even those who are producing a large amount of content—have never spent time thinking about the strategy for how they should release content to their audience. This is the best way to attract new customers and deepen the loyalties of your existing customers. And most important, it is the best way to keep your brand in the forefront of as many minds as possible. And front of mind equals tip of tongue.

Gone are the days when you could be just a product company or a content company. Today, you must be both. TOMS Shoes is a product company; but if you are a fan of its products, would you read its magazine? Would you watch its TV channel? Would you attend its events? Absolutely. National Geographic is a content company. But if you read their articles, would you be willing to buy a new line of outdoor gear from them? Probably.

A conversation about content often makes entrepreneurs nervous. That's because eventually you need to make money to sustain yourself with your start-up. Giving away free content seems counterintuitive to making money. But in the modern marketplace, the money is in the audience. It's in the platform, not the product. When you have people's attention, you can sell almost anything. And the more a follower consumes content by you, the more likely they are to buy something from you.

While loyalty is the goal, it's a slow burn. Falling in love with someone's story requires history, variety, and a well-rounded look at their life. In my experience, this meant producing an array of content. It meant buying a nice camera to share our story with high-quality visuals. It meant hiring a photographer a few times per year for new head shots, lifestyle photos, and visual aids to deepen the connection with followers. I knew my audience wouldn't make the equivalent of a life commitment after one date to Applebee's.

Of course, there is a big difference in this analogy. In relationships, you only have to ask someone to marry you once. In the marketplace, you have to propose again and again. Constantly asking your audience to spend money feels annoying and makes you seem like a beggar. It creates a relationship with your customer that is purely transactional. Imagine getting a news feed or e-mail at the start of every week saying, "Check out our new products" and three days later, "Check out our new products" and three days later "Check out our new products." I'm getting annoyed just typing it. That kind of strategy will get you an "unsubscribe" or an "unfollow" faster than a freight train.

If you want to build a successful start-up, take time and do it the right way. Building a solid relationship with your audience requires time. Finding your online voice requires time. But the sooner you can leverage your brand as a content platform to share your story in a useful and engaging manner, the sooner you'll have a community of people who trust you. And when people trust you, they will buy from you.

If you build a business the right way, your audience *will* come. Because by the time you launch it, they will already be there.

☑ COMPLETE DAY #10

☐ REMEMBER

People prefer to follow people, not businesses, brands, and blogs.
#LaunchYourDream

☐  ASK

Which social media platform do you believe will help you build an audience fastest? What's holding you back?

☐ BELIEVE

I have to build an audience *before* I build a business.

☐ DO

Come up with three article titles today that you will publish before you launch your start-up. Make sure that they align with your whyology and are useful to your customers.

DAY 11

Consistency Beats Frequency

Estimated Reading Time: 6 Minutes

For entrepreneurs, time is perhaps the only commodity more limited than money. The way they schedule their time, especially in the early days when they may still be working a day job, must be intentional for it to be effective. For this reason, after I talk to starters about content, they normally follow up by asking about frequency. How often should you post an article or podcast or engage on social media? Every day? Once per week? Only when you feel inspired?

I normally don't give them the answer they are looking for. In fact, I don't answer their question at all. Instead, I change the question. The most important part about building an audience with content is not frequency but consistency. If you disappear online, so will your audience.

Does this mean you have to work seven days per week? I don't think so. It would certainly go against my philosophy. But start-ups have to *appear* as if they exist without pause. You must learn to produce, publish, and share content regularly. This will often mean using apps and technology that will let you work ahead and schedule content into the future. But it must be appearing consistently.

People who have never started a business sometimes assume that those who run their own companies have the luxury of working only when they feel like it. I wish this were true, but it isn't. And that goes for blogging, social media, podcasting, and everything else we do online. Posting content is part of your job, which means you don't get to opt out if you don't feel the muse tapping your shoulder. Does a bricklayer get to stay in and read poetry until he feels like laying bricks? No. He rises each work-day and lays bricks because that is his job.

Ultimately it's more important to produce a few pieces of content per week with ruthless consistency than to produce lots of content one week and none the next. It's better to post once per day for seven days than two posts on Monday, none on Tuesday, three on Wednesday, and another on Saturday. The key is to find a pace that you can sustain. At the time of this writing, the pace that works for my family is an article of five hundred to one thousand words, one podcast, and a three- to five-minute video each week. I post one to three times per day across most social media platforms, six days a week.

Nobody likes an unintentional, disorganized, inconsistent friend. And when you're building a start-up, you're asking people to be your friend. To join you on the journey. To support you and participate in your story. The same emotions that apply to friend-ship building apply to audience building.

Consistency is not just about regularity either. You want to be consistent in your style. Consistent in your tone. Consistent in the topics you are covering and the imagery you're attaching to it. By offering a steady voice and approach to your content, you will remove the barriers between you and the people looking to offer you their loyalties. The brands with the most followers and highest engagement are not just those that post every day, but those with consistently styled content and an unchanging voice.

Of course, consistency comes at a cost. You will be required to mark out your style, be intentional about topic choice, and sometimes search longer for the right image. You will have to be diligent in producing content regularly and scheduling it to release on time. You may have to learn new software or applications that will make these jobs easier. And you have to work to share the content you post—a job that sometimes makes people uncomfortable.

There are two parts to regularly releasing content: creating it and distributing it. This means you need to share your content across social platforms after posting it and learn to write headlines that will engage your audience. It means sending a weekly e-mail to subscribers, alerting them to your new article, podcast, or video.

Distribution is less like shooting a rifle and more like skipping a rock. You should share it not just once, but multiple times. Too many people let great content sit in their archives after being seen only once by their audience. I'll share a popular article again and again—about every two months. Buzzfeed.com is one of the Internet's most popular websites. It produces thousands of articles each month. Three of its top five articles of all time are articles that were originally posted years ago. Buzzfeed changes the titles and images often and then re-shares them.

Brainstormed content that isn't produced content is wasted content. And produced content that isn't shared content is useless content. So learn to create consistently, and your start-up will be positioned for success.

☑ COMPLETE DAY #11

☐ REMEMBER

"Consistency is the true foundation of trust. Either keep your commitments or do not make them."

—Roy T. Bennett

ASK

How much time each day can you set aside for creating and distributing content?

☐ BELIEVE

I need momentum to build an audience, and I need consistency to build momentum.

DO

Define a sustainable content creation and distribution schedule that fits your lifestyle.

Be Pixel Perfect

DAY 12

Pointing You Somewhere

Estimated Reading Time: 11 Minutes

Launching a small start-up means being a tiny David standing alone in a field before a bigger, better corporate Goliath. Unlike the actual David, you'll need more than a stone and a sling to be successful. You're outmatched, outmanned, and out-funded. No need to phone the bookies in Vegas—we all know that the odds fall in the giant's favor.

Are you depressed yet? Well, you shouldn't be.

Thanks to the Internet, the battlefield has been somewhat leveled. While your competitor may have more stores and more billboards and more commercials than you, Goliath has the same amount of online real estate you do. Since Americans are increasingly using the Internet to research businesses and make purchases, that means the height gap between you and the big boy has been narrowed significantly. What are you going to do about it?

A start-up is dead on the field without a clear and compelling website: a starter cannot afford to just throw one together. Your website is where people come to learn about who you are, why you exist, and why they should give their money to you instead of the corporate Goliath.

If you've consumed much conventional wisdom about website construction, you'll be tempted to skip this chapter. While many modern business articles instruct entrepreneurs to outsource this portion of their business launch, they will do so at their peril. I prefer to live by the wisdom of the iconic designer Charles Eames, who once said, "Never delegate understanding." In today's economy, entrepreneurs don't have to know how to do everything, but they must *understand* how to do everything. When it comes to your website, you don't have to become a web designer. But you need to understand what good web design entails, so you can guide your designer in creating the website.

Because of the Internet's complexity, I could throw a million principles at you. And because the Internet is always changing, many of those principles would be obsolete by the time you learned them. If you've used the Internet long enough, you know how quickly website practices, design styles, and conversion strategies change. So I'll save you the time, tears, and frustration and focus instead on what is most important and most permanent.

Get a Goal

Designing a website is like flying a plane. You need all the right gear—working flaps, inflated tires, a full tank of gas. But the purpose of these tools is to get you somewhere. A plane without a flight plan, without a destination, might as well stay in the hangar.

I'm surprised by the number of entrepreneurs who design

a site but haven't set a specific goal for that site. They aren't flying a plane; they are flying a kite. No wonder they aren't getting anywhere. Before you start putting together your website, take time to determine what you want it to achieve; what you want it to communicate; what you hope people will do when they visit it. You can have more than one goal, but you need at least one goal. As business thinker Stephen Covey once said, "Begin with the end in mind."

What is the top goal you hope to achieve when someone visits your website?

Become a Fortune-Teller

In addition to your goals, you must consider the goals of those who will visit your site. What do *they* want? Great web design is the anticipation of users' desires. You need to become a fortune-teller, thinking into the future so that you can be a step ahead of your customer. Consumers are highly goal driven on the Web. They visit sites because there's something they want to accomplish—maybe even buy your product. The ultimate failure of a website is in failing to provide the information users are looking for.

This point is especially critical for those who are starting businesses. The first law of e-commerce is that if users cannot find the product, they cannot buy it either. What product information are your users going to be looking for when they visit? If that information is not readily available, you will lose the sale.

One example of not answering users' questions is the failure to list the price next to the corresponding products and services. Price is the most specific piece of information customers use to understand the nature of an offering. Not providing it makes people feel lost and reduces their understanding of a product line. Do not make a user click to find out how much the sale will cost them. And don't just post this information on the product page. Include it on your category pages, previews, thumbnails, and more. This information allows users to differentiate among products and click through to the most relevant ones. Also include clear information like shipping costs, size charts, or cancellation policies. If you don't anticipate and meet your users' needs, they'll move on to someone who will.

Once you answer users' questions, you also need to predict where users will go next and what they'll want when they get there. These transitions should be seamless and intuitive. On the Web, usability is a necessary condition for survival. If a website is difficult to use, people leave. If the home page fails to clearly state what a company offers and what users can do on the site, people leave. If users feel lost after clicking a button or two, they leave. If a website's information is hard to read or doesn't answer users' key questions, they leave. Notice a pattern here? Plenty of other websites are available, so leaving is the first line of defense when users encounter a difficulty.

Best practices call for spending about 10 percent of a design project's budget on usability. On average, this 10 percent will more than double a website's desired quality metrics. Think of doubling sales; doubling the number of registered users or customer leads; doubling comments; doubling likes, follows, or e-mails; or doubling any other desired goal for your start-up. If you're bad at math, let me help you: doubling means more visitors, engagement, and money for your start-up. (For a free technical tutorial on how to set up your start-up's website, visit StartupCamp.com/website.)

What information could you add to your site to make important information more readily available to your customers?

Speak Clearly and Concisely

If someone lands on your website for five seconds, would they know who you are and what you do? Make sure this information is accessible and understandable. Labels in your website's navigation and copy in its pages must be easy for visitors to understand. Use common words that visitors expect. Avoid long sentences. Avoid jargon. Elaborate sentences and fancy words force the temporal lobe of our brains to work harder.

A big word might make you sound smart, but it risks making the reader feel dumb. A reader who doubts himself is unlikely to take action. And you want to inspire action. So be simple and accessible in your writing. Copy that works well for "low literacy" users works well for everyone. It's not about dumbing it down; it's about using simple language that everyone can understand.

For content sites, if the type is too small or the font is abnormal, reading becomes a struggle, and again visitors leave. Sometimes important specifics are buried under a thick layer of marketese or tucked in a corner so they are never noticed. Since users don't have time to read everything, hidden information like this might as well not be there.

Ask yourself: What about my site sounds confusing for low-literacy users? Where can I simplify to make it more relatable?

Take Time to Test

You should be performing tests at every stage of the design and development process. If you have an existing website, you should test the old site first to identify the good parts to keep and the hurdles to cut that are causing users to stumble. You should test your competitors' designs to get data on a range of alternative interfaces that have similar features to yours. Don't spend money on a new website until you've done your homework.

Once you get a design and interface you like, have others test it to see if you missed something. Conduct a field study by going to a coffee shop and asking a few people to visit your site for one minute without any guidance. Afterward, ask them questions: What do we do? What do we sell? How does our product work? What confused you? Make sure that the people you are polling are similar to those in your core audience. People ask my opinion of their websites all the time, and while my opinion may be more valuable than some, it will never be more valuable than a group of real users in your customer demographic.

Finally, refine through multiple iterations the concepts that test best. Test each iteration. Then once you decide on and implement the final design, test it again. Subtle usability problems always creep in during implementation. These small tweaks may mean the difference between making $50,000 or $500,000 in your first year of business.

Building the bones of your website will give your start-up the structure it needs to sustain the weight of doing business in the Internet age. But man cannot live with bones alone. We need skin and clothes and, if you live in Oregon, maybe a good lumberjack beard. Once your site is solid, you need to make sure it is stunning too.

☑ COMPLETE DAY #12

☐ **REMEMBER**

"It's much easier to double your business by doubling your conversion rate than by doubling your traffic."
—Jeff Eisenberg

☐ **ASK**

All roads should lead to your top destination. How can you make your website point more users there?

☐ **BELIEVE**

If users get lost, it ends in a cost.

☐ **DO**

Visit five competitors' websites and write down your favorite feature of each one.

DAY 13

Brains and Beauty

Estimated Reading Time: 9 Minutes

One of the most helpful principles I teach entrepreneurs is also one of the most controversial: people don't refer ugly. In a visual culture, aesthetics matter. The way you look, the way your products look, and the way your website looks matter. We teach our children that "it is the inside that really counts," and this is true for life. But when it comes to business, the outside matters too. A lot.

We know this is true thanks to eye-tracking studies, which use infrared cameras to observe and record the eye movement of study participants viewing website screenshots. These studies show that people spend more time viewing the logo, navigation bar, main image, and social media links than they do the actual content.[1] Another study showed that consumers' feelings of mistrust or rejection result more from design-related complaints about the website than from actual content—by a margin of more than nine to one.[2] And if that doesn't intimidate you, consider this: a recent study found that it takes users a mere twentieth of a second to judge the visual appeal of your website. So you have about fifty milliseconds to make a good first impression.[3]

Modern consumers expect exceptional design. They just don't want to be associated with ugly brands and ugly products. They don't want to browse ugly websites. Everything from your headshot to your social media grammar has to be intentional and visually pleasing. While the inside may matter in real life, when it comes to the Internet, the inside is irrelevant if the outside is ugly. You may have a more compelling mission than the neighborhood soup kitchen, but no one will know it if you have an ugly website. You may have the most useful product since the invention of the butter knife, but no one will know it if you have an ugly website. Your online presence must have both brains and beauty.

Focusing on image sounds vain in the age of authenticity. So if this offends your sensibilities, you have my permission to take a moment, walk outside, and shout at the sky about how stupid you think it is that looks matter so much to consumers. When you get done blowing off steam, come back inside and learn these four critical components to building a beautiful website.

Killer Colors

In the 1930s, the German scientist Hedwig von Restorff discovered that when given a list of ten items, people remember items if they are colored differently from the others. This is because the occipital lobe of our brain is sensitive to visual differences, or "pattern interrupters." Years later, the web marketer Paras Chopra conducted experiments that showed how standout colors aren't just remembered more; they're clicked 60 percent more often.

Make sure to pick an "action color" for all of your links, buttons, and rollover effects. Make it a color that's distinct from the brand colors, and use the action color nowhere else but in the clickable items. Small intentional adjustments like this can create immediate change to your bottom line. And here's a fun fact: in color-based click studies, orange and yellow remain the highest performers.

When it comes to colors, make sure you use them consistently. Customers should not wonder whether different words, situations, or actions mean the same thing. Use the same button color for calls to action site-wide. Use the headline fonts only for headlines.

Intentional Images

The images on your site are as important as the words, and many websites are made up mostly of images. If you have bad photography, you have a bad website. Can your audience see themselves in the people presented on your site? What type of emotions do the images invoke? Make sure that your images feel consistent over time and across the site. Select the images for both content and quality. A stunning photo that fails to communicate your product, service, or brand is as bad as a photo that hits the messaging perfectly but is blurry or has poor resolution. Oh, and make sure you check the license on images you choose. If you don't have the legal ability to use the image the way you have, you might get slapped with financial penalties for misuse.

Lovely Logos

Today, the first time people see your logo is on a website. I can't give you a foolproof process to choosing the perfect logo for your start-up. But some basic guidelines exist.

- Your logo should be *timeless*, so it doesn't go out of style too quickly. Switching logos frequently is expensive and can create brand confusion.
- Your logo should be *memorable*, so that it lingers with your customers. You want customers to be able to draw your logo if asked, or at least be able to pick it out of a lineup.
- Your logo should be *versatile*, so that you can use it in different sizes and contexts. The images and words should be easy to decipher on both a billboard and a smartphone screen.
- Your logo should be *appealing*, so that your target audience likes it. This seems intuitive, but not every entrepreneur considers this. Take time to conduct visual tests with people in your target customer demographic to make sure it resonates.

Simple Styling

Entrepreneurs who aren't naturally design minded have a tendency to include every trick in the book, but the best websites are clean and simple. Users respond favorably to streamlined websites that aren't larded with irrelevant content. Web researchers say that users strongly prefer website designs that appear both simple and familiar. One study even showed that users who experienced sites as too complex or too unfamiliar perceived them to be ugly, whether they were or not.

Every extra unit of information on a website competes with the relevant units of information and diminishes their visibility. The fewer components you include, the more power each component contains. As Antoine de Saint-Exupéry said, "A designer knows he has achieved perfection not when there is nothing left to add, but when there is nothing left to take away."[4] Whether you are working with a designer or purchasing a premade template, opt for simple and straightforward.

Also, browsing a website should never feel like strolling through a used car lot. Remove anything that feels like an ad. Strip out anything that feels like spam. These elements will crowd your site and put users in a defensive posture as they sense you're trying to sell them something at every turn. Think about how to create beautiful ad content that is connected to your whyology and doesn't feel like it belongs on the windshield of a 1997 Mazda Miata.

When customers visit your website, they will ascribe value to you and your product. And this could have an effect on customers for years to come. Customers will either remember you as "the company with the ugly images" or "the business with the beautiful website and great content." The first kind of customer will likely never return, but the second type of customer will. And when they do, they'll probably make a purchase.

Your business is only as valuable as people perceive it to be. And visuals translate into value.

☑ COMPLETE DAY #13

☐ REMEMBER

"There are three responses to a piece of design—yes, no, and WOW! Wow is the one to aim for."
—Milton Glaser

☐ ASK

Which element listed above—colors, images, logo, styling—requires more attention than you've been giving it?

BELIEVE

When I invest in my visuals, I invest in my value.

☐ DO

Get three quotes from a photographer today for your start-up's website. (Think headshots, product shots, office images, etc.)

Build the Box

DAY 14

Making It Legal

Estimated Reading Time: 8 Minutes

In 2007, Hallmark stores released a greeting card with pop culture icon Paris Hilton's face and the phrase "That's hot" on the front. The company was promptly slapped with a lawsuit from Hilton's attorneys, who claimed it had infringed on her name and likeness. If Hallmark had done its homework, it would have discovered that Hilton had trademarked the phrase "That's hot." Instead, the company settled with Hilton for an undisclosed amount—probably a hefty six-figure payment.[1]

Legal matters matter. They may be boring, but if you fail to learn the rules and accidentally break one, it could cost you everything you've worked for. We'll jump back into the fun parts of launching a start-up soon, but today let's take a swift jog through yawn-town. (Disclaimer: This discussion is applicable only for residents of the United States. If you don't live in America, you'll need to research the laws in your home country.)

When it comes to business, remember this: if it isn't official, it's probably illegal. Many people in business today break the law, whether they realize it or not, and a lot of them get away with it.

But a small investment of time can get you up to speed on how to launch your company inside the legal guidelines. It's worth taking the time to do it. You can't put a price tag on a good night's sleep.

If you want to be a business owner, you need to follow the rules. If you're making money, you need to pay taxes on it. If you don't, you're guilty of tax evasion. And the government considers this a big deal. If you don't believe me, ask Al Capone. If you're paying taxes, that means you're receiving income. And if other people are paying you, that means you have liability. If you have not officially registered your business, then you are personally liable. If a disgruntled vendor decides to serve you with a lawsuit, it could attempt to seize your personal assets.

Before you register your business, you will need to determine what type of company you plan to start. Here are some choices, in order of popularity:

1. **Sole Proprietorship:** A sole proprietor is someone who owns an unincorporated business by him- or herself.
2. **Partnership:** A partnership is the relationship existing between two or more people who join to carry on a trade or business. Each person contributes money, property, labor, or skill and expects to share in the profits and losses of the business.
3. **Limited Liability Company:** A limited liability company (LLC) is a business structure allowed by state statute. A few types of businesses generally cannot be LLCs, such as banks and insurance companies. Each state may use different regulations, so check with your own state if you are interested in starting an LLC.
4. **Corporation ("C Corporation"):** In forming a corporation, prospective shareholders exchange money,

property, or both for the corporation's capital stock. A corporation generally takes the same deductions as a sole proprietorship to figure its taxable income, but a corporation can also take special deductions. For federal income tax purposes, a C corporation is recognized as a separate taxpaying entity. A corporation conducts business, realizes net income or loss, pays taxes, and distributes profits to shareholders. The profit of a corporation is taxed to the corporation when earned and then is taxed to the shareholders when distributed as dividends. This is called double taxation.

5. **Corporation ("S Corporation"):** S corporations are corporations that elect to pass corporate income, losses, deductions, and gains through to their shareholders for federal tax purposes. Shareholders of S corporations report the flow-through of income and losses on their personal tax returns and are assessed tax at their individual income tax rates. This allows S corporations to avoid double taxation on their corporate income.[2]

In a variation of the S corporation, a company can file a "doing business as" (DBA) name. StartupCamp.com is a DBA of Dale Partridge, Inc., which is an S corporation. In my experience, an S Corp offers you the most protection and the least tax liability of all available options. A DBA is an assumed name, so if you already have an established company and want to launch a new start-up with a different name under that company, you need to register it as a DBA.

The final consideration for your business, and perhaps the most important, is trademarking. We might say this is the—ahem—Hallmark point of this chapter. A trademark is any unique word, symbol, name, or device used to identify and distinguish the goods of one seller from the goods of another—think Nike's swoosh. A trademark allows the seller to protect what's trademarked from use and/or misuse by competitors while building brand loyalty among customers. Trademarks also help prevent confusion or manipulation of consumers, who come to associate distinct attributes with a distinct brand.

Too many entrepreneurs have been forced to change their company's name or rename a product because someone else trademarked it before they did. From a branding perspective, the following are assets that can be protected: logos, names, taglines, and packaging. However, these assets can be trademarked only if they meet certain qualifications. A word or phrase that's commonly used or already connected with another product or service in the same industry cannot be trademarked. For example, a generic term like *search engine* can't be trademarked, but a unique name, like *Google*, can be. And if your name is generic but used in an industry not typically related to the meaning of the term, you may be able to trademark it. A good example would be Apple.

I recommend starting off with a trademark search. You can do this by going to uspto.gov and using the trademark search function. If you aren't infringing on someone else and you don't want others to infringe on you, the best way to register a trademark is to go through the U.S. Patent and Trademark Office, which establishes ownership beyond a doubt.

Legal considerations are so important, it may be good to hire an attorney to help you navigate some of the tricky parts. If you break the law, you could end up paying a penalty, or if you're really unlucky, you'll be mailing your mom a "That's hot" Christmas card from the county jail.

☑ COMPLETE DAY #14

REMEMBER

"The Separation is in the preparation."

—Russell Wilson

ASK

Which entity do you think works best for your start-up?

BELIEVE

If my business is unofficial, my business is illegal.

DO

Perform a basic trademark search of your desired business name today at uspto.gov. If that name is not taken in your class, register it as soon as possible.

DAY 15

A Small Leak Sinks Big Ships

Estimated Reading Time: 7 Minutes

It takes money to make money. But once you make it, the difficult part is keeping it. Many entrepreneurs fail because they learn only how to do the first part.

To graduate from grade school, you had to learn Newton's law about every action having an equal and opposite reaction. Before you graduate from StartupCamp, you need to memorize another maxim. We'll call it Partridge's First Law of Start-up Dynamics: every financial decision has a financial consequence. Whenever you earn a dollar and before you spend a dime, stop to ask yourself how you can best steward that money. As Dave Ramsey said, "You must gain control of your money or the lack of it will forever control you."[1]

Financial stewardship begins with financial structure. Good money management doesn't happen by accident. Here are three basic components of a strong financial structure.

Business Bank Accounts

Setting up at least two bank accounts for your business is not optional. All of your revenue and payments should be run through a checking account. And then you should have a savings account where you are storing up emergency money for lean times. You need to work toward having three to six months of salary plus expenses in your savings account. As Warren Buffet said, "Do not save what is left after spending, but spend what is left after saving."

Business accounts are also important for liability purposes. Having them will reduce your risk. Without them, a potential lawsuit may result in the seizure of your personal assets. Plus, no bank will let you set up an account without proper documentation, so this is a good test for whether you have your ducks in a row.

Accounting Software

Do not attempt to keep track of your entire organization's finances through a disorganized collection of Excel spreadsheets clipped to your computer's desktop or paper notebooks that could vaporize in a fire. Invest in affordable but high-quality accounting software to track invoices and payables, file taxes, and process payroll. If you plan to sell products online, make sure you spend time researching the right payment gateway. (Visit StartupCamp.com/finance for a free list of trusted tools.)

Pay Yourself Well

By this, I don't mean to write yourself a fat check every month. I mean that you should pay yourself as an employee of the company rather than taking dividends or draws. While some accountants may advise differently, I believe it will simplify your tax preparation, and the automatic deposit feature keeps your income consistent.

A few months ago I was consulting with the founder of a subscription box company who had more than fifteen thousand people paying $20 per month. That's $300,000 per month in top-line revenue. He had a team of five people and a small office. I asked him how much he was paying himself. His response: zero. He was living on credit cards, racking up personal debt, causing financial arguments between him and his wife, and on edge about the life span of his company.

This poor guy made his successful venture into a financial stress case for no reason. He became the classic entrepreneurial martyr. It's more common than you assume. If you don't build in your salary from the very beginning, you'll end up creating a habit of spending and invest almost all your money in the business. Your employees will be proud, people will commend you for it, and you'll be broke.

—

This all may sound complicated, but you don't have to manage your finances forever. When your business begins to make more money, hire a low-cost bookkeeper for two to three hours per week to handle your accounting needs. This person should be able to keep the finances reconciled and help prepare everything you'll need to give your accountant come tax season.

Once your structure is in place, your financial system will basically run itself. You'll be free to make more money as the business hums along. Just keep in mind one financial principle: debt is a company killer. Seriously. Debt is a vicious murderer with a thirst for your business's blood. And worse, he is sneaky. He'll creep up on you when you're not watching and slit your start-up's throat. So do everything you can to keep him out of your life.

By *debt*, I'm not just referring to a million-dollar line of credit; I'm talking about a hundred-dollar balance on your American Express. If you can't pay cash, you can't afford it. And this is true no matter what the "it" is. As Benjamin Franklin said, "Beware of little expenses. A small leak will sink a great ship."

In a Gallup poll, 36 percent of small business owners said they are uncomfortable with how much debt their businesses carry. Forty-nine percent said they find it extremely difficult to manage their current debt.[2] Even though certain business models require taking on debt to capitalize on growth opportunities, looming debt can squeeze the joy out of being an entrepreneur.

If you're going to invest your life and time and money into launching a start-up, you might as well enjoy it. Learn to make money, save money, and keep money, and you'll be free to enjoy your money for the rest of your life.

☑ COMPLETE DAY #15

☐ REMEMBER

"Too many business owners run into debt just to keep up with competitors who are already there."
#LaunchYourDream

☐ ASK

What about managing your money do you find most difficult?

☐ BELIEVE

I'll never be successful until I learn to successfully manage my money.

☐ DO

Spend thirty minutes researching to find the bank, accounting software, and payment gateway that will work for your start-up.

DAY 16

Money in Your Sleep

Estimated Reading Time: 8 Minutes

An entrepreneur named Michael Simmons published an article at *Forbes* that opened with two of the truest and saddest sentences I have ever read: "There is a persistent, unspoken belief that entrepreneurs must work 70–100 hours per week in order to be successful. In fact, this is often glorified."[1]

He's right. Many friends of mine who have started businesses brag about their brutal workdays and seven-day workweeks. I find this disturbing. Every entrepreneur should be figuring out how to work fewer hours while making more money. If you launched your business a decade ago and you're still slaving at the office sixty hours per week, you shouldn't be bragging. You should be embarrassed.

There was a time in history when becoming an entrepreneur was akin to a slave sentence. If you started a T-shirt store in the 1970s, you were forced to pay hefty rent for a storefront and needed to work long hours to keep the lights on. When your business wasn't open, you weren't making money. The longer you worked, the larger your paycheck would be. But our generation has been given the gift that previous generations haven't had: the Internet. If I started a T-shirt business today, my business could remain open without anyone being there to run the cash register.

Your goal should be to find a way to make money while you sleep. When I woke up this morning, I checked my account to see how many people paid their monthly dues to StartupCamp.com last night. I received thirty-two payments while I was snoring, including a new customer in Australia who spent $1,000 on one of our enrollment packages. This method of making money would not have been possible fifty years ago.

Most entrepreneurs never achieve this reality because they don't plan for it. They pay their entrance dues without developing an exit strategy. The best start-ups will progress through a three-stage life cycle:

Profit Dependent → People Dependent → Process Dependent

When a company starts, it is always profit dependent. It needs every dollar it can muster to pay the rent (and the entrepreneur's rent). But as it grows, it will become people dependent. The entrepreneur hires additional employees, but the team is small, so each role is critical. The business will be successful in this phase so long as all the right people are in place. This includes the entrepreneur—if these people step out, the whole deck of cards will collapse. Most start-ups never progress to the third stage, in which the company becomes process dependent. In that stage, your company is driven by the systems you've put into place. At this point, you're able to step away. If someone leaves, you'll eventually hire another person for their role. But meanwhile, the business keeps running. I'm not saying you need to get there immediately, but you should set your sights on this stage from day one.

The way this life cycle works is through multiplication. If a business owner hires fifty employees, fifty people are now pushing the company's mission and vision. There is no reason the owner and these employees should be carrying the same weight of the organization as multiplication occurs. Over time, they should delegate responsibilities and duplicate roles, letting multiplication happen naturally. Every component added to the equation is a way to replace yourself: an assistant is a multiplier; a scheduling app is a multiplier; a bookkeeper is a multiplier.

Too many people add employees without letting multiplication happen. They think they own their own company—but their company owns them. Rather than becoming entrepreneurs, they have become merchants or freelancers. They've created for themselves a job, not a company. True entrepreneurs will work to scale their organization so that its success is not directly related to the number of hours they work.

Here are four rules to live by if you want to become a process-dependent company that enables you to step away and make money in your sleep.

1. **Always Be Working Yourself Out of a Job:** Kill the perfectionism that is holding you back. Hire people better than you. If someone can get a job done 90 percent as well as you can while you're at the beach, that's a pretty good deal. Release the responsibility.
2. **If You Have a Product, Turn It into a Service:** Service businesses are admittedly harder to scale because you begin to accept that you can make only as much money as you have man-hours. But it is still possible. If you work hard to provide your service hundreds of times a year, ask yourself this question: "How can I package my service into a product and sell it by the thousands?"

StartupCamp.com is a great example of this approach. If I were a business coach who had to be physically present to train entrepreneurs, I'd have a ceiling on my salary. But by packaging my service into a product, I have shifted the equation.

3. **If You Have a Business Model, Turn It into a Membership Model:** If your business provides a service to customers, think about changing this into a subscription service. You offer an incentive in exchange for consistency, and everyone wins. If you own a coffee shop, provide a discount for people who will commit to a monthly membership that includes delivering a bag of coffee right to their doorstep at a reduced rate.

   I went to my barber recently, and he told me that his shop had developed a subscription plan. If I purchased my haircuts for an entire year at once, I received a five-dollar discount on each cut and a free beer whenever I came in. I got sixty bucks and twelve beers, and he got my loyalty and guaranteed revenue.

4. **Open an Online Store:** Unless you are a twenty-four-hour fitness center, your physical location is restricted by its hours of operations. If you own a brick-and-mortar shop, you have no excuse not to operate an online store too. This system can work even for service-based companies. If you own a landscaping company, you should sell outdoor tools and gardening guidebooks on your site.

   Most entrepreneurs are trying to find time to get some sleep. They should be focused on finding a way to make money while they sleep. By focusing on the latter, they'll achieve the former too.

☑ COMPLETE DAY #16

☐ REMEMBER

"If you don't find a way to make money while you sleep, you will work until you die."
—Warren Buffett

☐ ASK

What part of your job do you see as being difficult for you to release?

☐ BELIEVE

I want to make more money in less time, not the other way around.

☐ DO

Write down three ways you can systematize your company to free up your time.

Launch Loud

DAY 17

Once in a Lifetime

Estimated Reading Time: 10 Minutes

Each year in the global marketplace, there are as many as 250,000 major product launches.[1] That's more than 680 products per day and nearly one new product every two minutes. Can you name even one of them? Probably not. Because as many as 95 percent of new products fail each year.[2] Most products launch like a rocket and drop like a rock.

According to Joan Schneider and Julie Hall, authors of *The Launch Plan*, the biggest reason that products fail is lack of preparation. "Companies are so focused on designing and manufacturing new products that they postpone the hard work of getting ready to market them until too late in the game," they say.[3] A product failure usually results from a planning failure.

Even though your start-up launch may still be weeks away, the preparation has already begun. You get only one chance to launch your start-up. With so many products failing each year, the odds are not in your favor. The planning you do now will determine which side of the statistics you end up on.

When I released my first book, *People Over Profit*, I began preparing about six months before the launch date. I studied other successful book campaigns to gather creative ideas. I met with a few of my strategic friends to host a brainstorming session. I called book-marketing consultants to harvest wisdom over the phone. From this, I compiled a to-do list of 155 prelaunch tasks. With so much to do in the preparation phase, every starter needs a launch plan to make sure nothing falls through the cracks. Don't fool yourself into believing a launch can happen without a written plan of concrete ideas, deadlines, tasks, delegation of responsibility, expected results, and a backup plan in case plan A falters. (To download a copy of the *People Over Profit* launch plan, visit StartupCamp.com/launch-plan.)

Here are seven critical questions that must be answered as you plan for your big day:

1. Is Your Customer Right?

   Launching a product without understanding its intended customer is like shooting an arrow without picking a target. Once you know the demographic you want to attract, conduct a customer survey. Ask strangers in that demographic about your potential product. Maybe even conduct some low-cost market research from a local college. You don't know what you don't know. And what you don't know can ruin your launch.
2. Is the Timing Right?

   The moment you launch will often determine the momentum of your launch. A good product launched at a bad time usually fails. If you launch a new school supply product in April, for example, don't expect it to take off. Students are not in the market for supplies at the end of their last semester. Or if you launch a product targeted to moms a week before Mother's Day, you've missed your window for the strongest selling season. Make sure that you're not missing an opportunity because you haven't consulted a calendar.

3. Is Your Timeline Right?

   Once you've chosen the launch date, make sure you have enough time to execute each step in your launch plan before that day arrives. Rushing a launch is a good way to ruin it. As Bob Shelton, a forty-year retail veteran and longtime Safeway merchandising executive said, "Sometimes going slow to go fast can help you make adjustments to strategy and marketing on the fly by establishing well-measured, goal-oriented checkpoints in time."[4]

   The internal stage of your launch can begin as far out as you deem necessary. But the public portion should not be more than three months before the launch date. In my experience, any further out means the product feels stale when it should feel fresh. Humans don't have the capacity to remember to purchase a product you told them about a year ago. So plant seeds on social media, your blog, and through advertising; but be sure to do it no more than ninety days out. Publicly set a deadline to keep yourself accountable, knowing that if you miss it, you'll blow your credibility.

4. Is Your Team Right?

   As I've said, it takes a village to launch a start-up. You will need many hands to lift your business to success. Make sure to evaluate the support mechanism behind your product. Do you have your marketing materials in order? Has the packaging been tested? Is your back-end system functioning properly? Have you developed a plan for gathering metrics and feedback? If you answered no to any of those questions, you may need to return to question 3 and delay your launch.

5. Is Your Product Right?

   Despite all the technological advances of the twenty-first century, word-of-mouth marketing is still one of the most effective ways to propel a product to success. The last thing you want is to flawlessly execute a launch plan, have two hundred people purchase your product, and then have 50 percent of them write negative reviews. Make sure your product fulfills your promise.

   When you get your product right, you must also make sure you get your price point right. Most entrepreneurs fear they will fail due to overpricing their product. Ironically, many fail because of the exact opposite. Due to their low self-confidence, they underprice their product instead. You may think, *That sounds like a great problem. A lower price point leads to more sales, right?* Not always. In the market, people associate an excessively cheap price with an excessively cheap product. If your price point is too high, you can stunt sales. But make sure you don't fail in the other direction. To find the perfect price point, look for three competing products and make sure you are within range. If you decide to price your product outside of that margin anyway, you better have ironclad reasoning for making that decision.
6. Is Your Goal Right?

   A plan without a goal is just a wish. For my first book launch, I set a goal of ten thousand copies presold by launch day. It took nearly all 155 action steps to hit that number. If you're setting an aggressive goal for your launch, make sure you have an equally aggressive strategy. Offering pricing incentives or giveaways for early orders can also be helpful. If you have some launch capital, consider producing a professional video, five-star product photography, and even a physical prototype. With the growth of crowdfunding sites like Kickstarter, going with a preorder strategy can dramatically lower the risk of a launch. Automobile manufacturer Tesla launched a preorder campaign for a coming model and reserved more than 400,000 units. This plan generated billions of dollars in implied sales.

7. Is Your Publicity Right?

   If you launch the most amazing start-up in the history of start-ups, it will not matter if no one hears about it. Contact online influencers and relevant members of the press to alert them. Craft a social media strategy for your raving fans. If you're buying advertising, consider the best places to invest money.

—

Once you've completed all of the actions on your list, you should add one more item: plan a party. With all of this hard work, you will need to celebrate your team, yourself, and everything you've accomplished. As the great president Abraham Lincoln once said, "Give me six hours to chop down a tree and I will spend the first five sharpening the axe." He's right. But once the tree has fallen, take a moment to savor its fruit.

Celebration is also important because launching your start-up is only the beginning. It is the first day of a long stint of hard work. Many entrepreneurs think about their launch date like the Super Bowl, but it's more like the opening game of a very long season.

☑ COMPLETE DAY #17

☐  **REMEMBER**

"Launch day is less like the Super Bowl and more like the first game of the season."
#LaunchYourDream

☐ **ASK**

What day do you want to launch your start-up and why?

☐  **BELIEVE**

The success of my launch is built on the strength of my planning.

☐ **DO**

Create the first draft of your comprehensive launch plan today. Include at least twenty-five steps.

DAY 18

Building Smart into Your Start

Estimated Reading Time: 15 Minutes

What makes customers move in the marketplace? What causes them to click a link, hand over their e-mail addresses, purchase a product, or sign up for a service? Many new entrepreneurs assume customers move because of information. They imagine customers weighing the options, evaluating the price, sketching a pros and cons list, and then making the most logical decision. You probably don't make marketplace decisions this way, so why would you assume that your customers do?

Emotions make a customer move. They click, divulge, purchase, or sign up primarily because of inspiration, not information. As Geoffrey James, contributing editor to *Inc.* magazine wrote, "Buying decisions are *always* the result of a change in the customer's emotional state. While information may help change that emotional state, it's the emotion that's important, not the information."[1]

Why is this significant for starters to know? Because American families, on average, repeatedly buy the same 150 items, which constitute as much as 85 percent of their household needs.[2] If your product is going to succeed, you need to break into a family's routine. You need to interrupt your customers' habits. This means prying their hands off the products they're already spending their money on and convincing them to spend their money with you instead. The only way to do this is to create a disruptive emotional trigger in your customers that makes them move.

Here are six proven triggers that can propel your start-up to success.

People Move When They Feel Excited

One of the best ways to launch strong is to build a sense of anticipation. Have you ever wondered why the Internet breaks every time Apple rolls out new products at its worldwide developers conference? And have you ever wondered why people stand in line for hours the day a new iPhone or MacBook arrives—even though they could waltz back into the store a week later and purchase it in ten minutes? Why can't they wait? Because they are *excited*.

Good entrepreneurs know how to build a sense of anticipation. Anticipation creates demand. And demand generates sales.

Before you launch, make sure you announce the launch date. This will help set customers' sights on a specific time when they can engage with your goods or services. Put a countdown clock on your site, and make your product available early to influencers and members of the press. Then provide aspiring buyers with specific instructions for what they need to do. For example, "arrive at 6 a.m." or "place your order by midnight" or "use this hashtag to enter." Then combine the specificity with curiosity, and you'll generate excitement.

This is what Blake Mycoskie, founder of TOMS Shoes, did when he sent padlocked, six-foot-tall wooden tubes to every Nordstrom store in North America. Inside was a brand-new TOMS product that nobody had ever seen. These tubes sat in stores for two weeks while managers, employees, and customers walked past a giant sign that declared, "The Next TOMS Product Will Change Everything" and had a reveal date posted below. When the date came, the doors were opened and the new TOMS sunglass line was unveiled. Because customers were excited, they bought pairs in droves.

People Move When They Feel Affection

Customers say yes to people, products, and brands they like. The principle is so simple and self-evident, it is almost silly to mention. Think about it. Do you give your money to people and causes that you loathe? No, you don't. If you want people to move toward your start-up, you need to generate feelings of affection toward your start-up.

What causes a person to feel affection? Persuasion science reveals at least three important factors:

1. We like people who are similar to us. At the most basic level, this means that companies need to feel more human. At a deeper level, this means companies need to feel more like the kind of humans they seek to serve. If you want to attract customers, your start-up needs to look and feel similar to them. Faceless companies—businesses without a visible leader—often fail because customers perceive such companies as lacking a soul.
2. We like people who pay us compliments. Who doesn't like to feel good about themselves? We all do. And we

naturally gravitate toward those who praise us. If you want to attract customers, your start-up needs to encourage and affirm them.

3. We like people who share our goals. This point conjures up the importance of your start-up's *why*. People move when they connect with your mission and purpose and vision. If you want to attract customers, convince them to fall in love with what you stand for.

People Move When They Feel Obligated

When you give something to people, those people often feel they should give back to you. That's the way humans are designed. If a friend invites you to her party this week, you feel obligated to invite her to your party next week. If a colleague does you a favor this week and asks you for a favor next week, you feel obligated to say yes. One way to get people to move in the marketplace is to give them something before you ask them for something.

In business terms, this transaction is called reciprocity, which should not be confused with generosity. The definition of *generosity* is to give and expect nothing in return. The definition of *reciprocity* is to give in hopes of receiving something in return.

I leveraged this tactic during the launch for my book *People Over Profit* by offering five hundred people a free paperback version of my book before it was available for purchase. I paid for the shipping cost of each unit. All I asked was for them to read the book, leave a review on Amazon, fulfill a few promotion tasks leading up to launch week, and join my private online group. By giving them something for free, I leveraged a small army to support my launch. And it worked. We had over 100,000 shares on social media, we trended on Twitter, built hype online, got lots of positive reviews within the first week, and many of those same supporters went to the store and bought a copy too.

Think of this like billions of little bank accounts—one for every person on earth. When you do something for someone else, you make a deposit into their favor bank. They feel that deposit. They know they have a positive balance. They know the money came from you. When you go to withdraw the deposit later, they feel obligated to give it back to you. In the months leading up to your launch, you want to make a lot of deposits in other people's favor banks. Maybe you write a blog about a friend who has a large following on social media, or you send a gift to someone you'll eventually be asking for an endorsement. When it comes time to withdraw your funds, you won't be left empty-handed.

People Move When They Feel Invested

When you launch a start-up, you're asking people to invest their time and hard-earned money in something that is essentially unproven. This is quite an obstacle to overcome, but it is not impossible. The best way to overcome it is to ask them to commit to something small first. This step will make your customers feel invested. And when they feel invested, they are more likely to take the next step out of consistency. People like to be consistent with what they have previously said or done.

My new hometown of Bend, Oregon, has a slogan: "Keep Bend Local." Imagine that I worked for the city and set a goal of having one out of every ten citizens in Bend purchase a yard sign with our town's slogan on it. Rather than asking people to spend the money for the yard sign right away, I might go around town selling "Keep Bend Local" automobile window clings for a quarter. If they agree to do something small, they are more likely to say yes when you ask them to purchase the yard sign. Why? Because it removes the guesswork about where my customers live. Since they've already publicly committed to the idea, my request feels consistent with who they are.

People Move When They Feel Comfortable

One of the most valuable emotions in the marketplace is trust. If people trust you, they are more likely to give you the things they value—from their time to their paycheck. One of the best ways to make people feel comfortable and build trust is to create a sense of authority.

Think about the way you relate to police officers. They wear uniforms and badges not only so you can identify them as police officers, but also because those items convey authority. And because we see them as people with authority, most of us trust them. Because we trust them, we feel comfortable around them. When they speak, we listen. When they tell us to do something, we obey. When we see them, we automatically feel something that makes us respond to them in a certain way.

The same is true with your website and marketing materials. The images you portray and words you use can give a sense of authority and build trust. Or they can undermine both. Apple knows this, which is why it calls its customer service technicians "geniuses." You're more likely to see a genius as a person of authority and trust that person with your device or money.

One way to build authority is through validation. I have often used this tactic on my businesses' websites. Potential customers find endorsements from prominent, successful businesspeople who tell them that they can trust me. Customers then reason that if this many people or that kind of person will vouch for me, then I must be trustworthy. There is a reason I asked Dave Ramsey and Mark Burnett to give endorsements. And for more credibility, I even added a counter on my blog that shows exactly how many people have subscribed to my e-mail list and how many people follow me on my social media profiles. When people feel uncertain, they look to the actions and behaviors of others to determine their own.

People Move When They Feel Exclusive

Everyone likes to feel special. They like to be the first ones in line or the only ones in line or to know about a line that no one else knows exists. They like to buy items when there is a limited supply. If you make people believe that the product or service you are selling is scarce, then they will feel exclusive. When they feel exclusive, they are more likely to move.

In 2014 I launched an online event called "Blogcamp." But rather than let anyone purchase tickets, we made people apply. This drove people nuts. But it drove applications through the roof. We had more than six hundred applicants. Since the event wasn't open to the public, the attendees felt special because they were chosen. We added another dimension with the pricing structure. People could purchase one of three packages: $79, $99, and $149. I made it clear that if customers wanted all the information and content, they would need to purchase the largest package. But there was a limited supply at this level, and we had only 150 spaces. What happened? The $149 packages sold out first.

Amazon will often tell you there are only six items left in stock, so "order soon." It's not going to sell out, but you feel as though it might. So you buy. Threadless.com lists how many shirts of each size are left in stock. This makes you feel a sense of urgency, and you're more likely to buy. Simply put, people want more of those things they can have less of.

You're getting ready to launch your start-up into the world. Make sure you start smart. Keep these principles front and center leading up to the launch date, and then keep them close by for the rest of your career. The same principles that guide your launch can help you plan your tenth anniversary celebration.

You're welcome.

☑ COMPLETE DAY #18

☐ REMEMBER

"Speak to people how they need to hear it, not how you want to say it."
#LaunchYourDream

☐ ASK

Which emotion do you think is most powerful for your customers, and which brands have you seen appeal well to that emotion?

BELIEVE

To be a great starter, I must communicate smarter.

☐ DO

List one way you can incorporate each of the six emotions into the first month after launch.

DAY 19

A Talkable Experience

Estimated Reading Time: 8 Minutes

A little more than 120 miles from where I live is a town named Eugene, Oregon. It's known as the home of the state's largest university, but it is also where you'll find the headquarters of Coconut Bliss, a dairy-free alternative dessert. Currently, Coconut Bliss distributes more than two million pints of its product across America annually. The company's success is not due to a massive influx of investor capital or a multimillion-dollar advertising campaign. It has grown primarily through word-of-mouth marketing.

When Coconut Bliss enters a new market, it holds local tasting parties where potential customers can sample its product. These events generate interest among the masses, and Coconut Bliss then asks them to petition local retailers to carry its products. Its social media team is adept at telling great stories about happy customers in highly shareable formats. As a result, this company started small but has reaped huge profits.

Coconut Bliss is one of many companies that have built their success on the bedrock of word-of-mouth marketing. Starbucks, Chipotle, Red Bull, and Zappos are other companies that have implemented similar strategies. Word-of-mouth marketing is an affordable, time-tested tactic that all entrepreneurs can use to grow their start-ups.

People love to share stories, news, and information with those around them. We tell our friends about great vacation destinations, books we read, and good deals we find. We write online reviews about restaurants, we share rumors, and we tweet about articles we agree with. People share more than sixteen thousand words per day, and every hour more than 100 million conversations about brands are happening online. The things others tell us, e-mail us, and text us have a significant impact on what we think, read, buy, and do. We try coffee shops our neighbors recommend, visit blogs our relatives praise, and vote for candidates our friends endorse.

That's why word of mouth remains one of the most effective forms of marketing. More than nine in ten consumers trust recommendations from family members and friends over all other forms of advertising, according to Nielsen.[1] Given that it is so useful, every entrepreneur probably uses it effectively, right? Wrong. According to a recent study by the American Marketing Association, 64 percent of marketing executives recognize that word of mouth is the most effective form of marketing, but a tiny 6 percent of them say they have mastered it.[2]

Many entrepreneurs stumble by focusing their marketing efforts on collecting instead of connecting. Brands often become so caught up in collecting social media fans, they forget to actually connect with them. Having a hundred really passionate fans who love your brand or product is exponentially more effective than having ten thousand "fans" who signed up just to win a free iPad from you. As I often say, making friends online is a lot like making friends in real life. If you have to purchase your friends, how committed can you really expect them to be?

When it comes to word-of-mouth marketing, the secret to winning is based on the three *E*'s: engage, equip, empower:[3]

Engage

The best gift you can give potential customers is you. Make sure you're engaging with them often and deeply. Listen to what they are telling you. Talk to them like human beings. Become a part of the conversation about your brand.

Most large corporations now have customer service accounts on social media run by real people to serve their customer bases more effectively. When you experience an airline nightmare, you can usually post at your carrier and get a real response. When the teams manning these accounts turn a terrible tale into a happy ending, the same people who were slaying them online begin praising them instead. If you watch the replies section, they are filled with responses to followers. Every few minutes, you can watch them respond to someone new. The result is an army of talkative fans recommending your brand with joy.

Equip

Your customers won't talk unless you give them something to say. Think about the content you'd like your fans to share and then equip them with highly shareable stories, videos, and graphics and the right language. This might be amazing products, remarkable customer service stories, insider knowledge, social elevation, unbelievable facts, or even funny disclosures.

Apple has revolutionized the tech industry by delivering amazing products to its consumers. The company wraps a new iPhone in a beautiful box, so that customers choose to take and post pictures of their new products rather than ditching the packaging. A creative customer experience equips people naturally to share, suggest, and refer their friends. Remember, people suggest only beauty. They never refer ugly. The way your business looks, feels, and acts must be nothing short of magnificent for the equip strategy to work.

Empower

If you equip your customers, you need to clearly ask them to engage in a desired action. If you do this on social media, make sure you know the proper etiquette for asking on that network. If you ask in the wrong way, your customers won't perceive it as empowerment, but as exploitation.

A great empowerment tool is to provide a concierge service. While you can create amazing experiences for every customer, you can do something truly special for a select few. Do something for some that you wish you could do for all. Target a few influential customers and dream up something so incredible, they can't help telling their friends about it. A generous affiliate or referral program gives them a motive to find ways for sharing within their community.

You don't have to put all of your eggs into word-of-mouth marketing, but you can't afford to leave that basket empty. When people share their positive opinions, it will make a difference in achieving your mission. If you can get people talking and give them something amazing to say, you'll harness the world's oldest marketing mechanism and unleash the power of positive press.

☑ COMPLETE DAY #19

☐ **REMEMBER**

"Do what you do so well that people can't resist telling others about you."

—Walt Disney

☐ **ASK**

In a perfect future, what would be the most common opinion people would share about your start-up?

☐ **BELIEVE**

When I collect a customer, I should connect with a customer.

☐ **DO**

Craft one sentence that you want your customers to use when describing your start-up to their friends.

Sell the Story

DAY 20

You're Not the Hero

Estimated Reading Time: 9 Minutes

On January 24, 1984, Steve Jobs had the task of presenting the first Mac computer to the world. He did so without the benefit of presentation software, which hadn't yet been invented. Instead of mesmerizing the crowd with beautifully designed graphic slides, he walked onto the stage and told an amazing story. It was filled with heroes and villains, impending defeat and ultimate victory. His speech is still considered one of the greatest presentations in modern business history, and it revolutionized the way many entrepreneurs think about business.[1] Why? Because he reminded these stat-focused managers that story is the ultimate building block of life and business.

As Rodger Dean Duncan of *Forbes* wrote, "No doubt about it, the best speakers are good storytellers. The best writers are good storytellers. The best leaders are good storytellers. The best teachers and trainers and coaches are good storytellers. It might even be argued that the best parents are good storytellers. While storytelling is not the only way to engage people with your ideas, it's certainly a critical part of the recipe."[2]

Your organization is telling a story whether you realize it or not, and you are a character in that tale. If you want to launch a successful start-up, you need to recognize which type of story you are telling and which character role you are filling.

In Christopher Booker's *The Seven Basic Plots*, he shows readers that all stories derive from only a handful of types—from rags to riches and overcoming the monster to voyage and return and rebirth to something new.[3] But these stories usually follow one meta-story that begins with an anticipation stage in which the hero is called to the adventure. This is followed by a dream stage in which the adventure commences, the hero has some success, and an illusion of invincibility emerges. This is then followed by a frustration stage in which the hero confronts the enemy for the first time, and the illusion of invincibility vanishes. This worsens in the nightmare stage, which is the climax of the plot, where hope is apparently lost. Finally, in the resolution, the hero overcomes his or her burden in the face of all odds.

The reason Hollywood makes so much money is that moviemakers have learned to exploit this meta-story to appeal to the way the human mind works. They make you feel that you can relate to the hero—that you *are* a hero. This allows them to attract, excite, and drive people. The best brands intuitively understand this appeal. They tell a story with intention so that their customers are inspired by it and swept into it.

You need to look at the story your start-up is telling and understand how you can position your brand in a plot that drives the same emotions you experience when watching your favorite movie. And this begins by identifying which character you are and which ones you are not. If you believe you are playing the wrong character, then you are telling the wrong story.

My friend Donald Miller, a bestselling author and genius corporate coach, has revolutionized the way businesses tell their stories by popularizing these ideas. He points out that most entrepreneurs hamstring their organizations because they believe *they* are the heroes.[4] But as Donald often reminds people, "You are not Luke Skywalker. You're Yoda." And Yoda is another type of character that people often overlook: the guide.

What's the difference?

- Heroes are flawed and filled with doubt. They are forced into action and taken on a quest, which causes them pain. Somewhere in the story, they recognize the need for a guide, and the guide helps them overcome whatever they are facing.
- Guides are experienced "experts" who, once upon a time, were heroes. They want the hero to win, provide a clear path forward, and participate in the hero's transformation by providing tools or "weapons" that lead to victory. A guide doesn't hog the credit but is willing to take responsibility.

What does this look like, practically speaking?

If you're launching an innovative health insurance brokerage firm, you might tell a story about a small-business owner (hero) who gets a call from the "evil" health insurance corporation (villain) informing him that premiums for his small business are about to shoot through the roof. This creates a problem for the hero, who calls you (guide). You provide the hero with information about innovative solutions that are low cost and will meet all of his company's needs. The hero phones the villain and tells him his services are no longer needed. Victory!

Another example might be a student (hero) who is trying to type a paper so she can graduate from college. Her poor-quality computer is broken, and the manufacturer's customer service department (villain) refuses to help. She stumbles across your business (guide), which refurbishes computers. You provide a cheap service so the hero can shake off the villain, finish the paper, and graduate on time. Victory!

Are you starting to understand? There is a subtle difference between stories in which you are the hero and those where your customer is the hero, but the difference pays off. You are not Frodo; you're Gandalf. You're not Harry Potter; you're Dumbledore. When you get this right, your potential customers will see themselves in the stories you tell about your existing customers and be moved to hire you or purchase your product too.

Also remember that nothing fuels a story quite like hope. Every hero has a problem. And every problem must be overcome. What's the tension your heroes experience most often? Who are the villains they usually encounter? How can you help them become victorious? Make sure you can describe in a simple way the negative consequences your customers may experience if they fail to follow your path. And communicate clearly the victory you can deliver if they heed your advice. This approach creates a clear call to action that will empower the hero to save the day with your help.

The bar is high when it comes to telling your story, but these tools can become your ladder. So take time to master them. If you learn to tell better tales and spin better stories, your start-up is more likely to experience a "happily ever after."

☑ COMPLETE DAY #20

☐ **REMEMBER**

"Don't tell them; show them."

#LaunchYourDream

☐ **ASK**

Which companies have been guides for you when you faced a perilous problem?

☐ **BELIEVE**

My customers don't need a hero; they need a guide.

☐ **DO**

Write out your start-up's story as if you were penning the plot of a Hollywood blockbuster. Who is the hero? The villain? The guide? What is the hero's problem, and how will he or she achieve victory?

DAY 21

Wordsmith Wonders

Estimated Reading Time: 10 Minutes

Most entrepreneurs I know weren't creative writing majors in college. In fact, some haven't read anything in a year apart from a handful of business and leadership books, and they write almost nothing. This is a problem because they are often subpar writers when they need to be stellar writers. For this reason, most starters should invest some time and energy in becoming better at writing copy.

Every marketing piece you'll ever produce, every website you'll ever help design, every advertisement you'll ever approve, every blog you'll ever release—every one of these items will consist of some combination of three elements: words, colors, and images. Of these three items, words are the most specific way to communicate your business messages, because only words have the ability to stand alone. And many entrepreneurs are weakest in the area of using words well. They know how to sell you a mattress using its dimensions and average customer review ratings, but they don't know how to use beautiful words to sell a good night's sleep.

Poetry has been defined as "the best words in the best order." Compelling copywriting follows the same definition. How can you arrange the best words in the optimal order to sell your product or service and convince prospective customers to take action? Here are four foundations of good copywriting that will take your start-up to the next level.

Amplify Existing Feelings

Imagine you're watching your favorite football team, and the quarterback gets injured. The replay video shows the linebacker exploiting a hole and pushing the quarterback to the ground. On the way down, his knee bends backward and pops out of the socket. His calf crumples, and you can see him reach for the leg out of pain. While watching the video, you cringe—over and over and over.

Or, suppose your best friend e-mails you a YouTube link to a video of a baby—so sweet and innocent in his pale blue onesie. The baby is crawling around a corner when his giant daddy jumps out and startles him. The baby falls back onto his butt in shock, pauses, and turns to the camera with a pitiful face; he starts whimpering and soon breaks into wails. You find yourself audibly responding, "Awwwwww!"

The biology behind this response depends on mirror neurons, which fire when we see someone act and mimic their reaction. According to research, these mirror neurons activate when you observe something happening and the feeling transfers onto you. That's why we speak back to the television or computer screen. God likely designed these neurons for a purpose—to bolster our sense of empathy or "walking in someone else's shoes."

Although most of the current research on mirror neurons

focuses on literal observation rather than words, great writers have the power to use words to force their readers to visualize the subject they are describing. The best writers can make readers speak back to them too as they feel what is being described. Think about my first example. Did you cringe at the thought of a man ripping the tendons in his leg? Good. You're already experiencing this effect in action.

When you're writing for your start-up, make people feel the emotions of the stories you're telling. Don't tell them what they should feel with leading phrases like "Doesn't that make you mad?" Instead, use words to make them feel the anger boil up in their blood.

If you're selling software that takes the hassle out of content optimization, you need to speak to the frustrated customer's feelings. He's tired of nitpicking and game playing for Google. He's exhausted from looking for a solution, and he just wants to do what he does best. If you're selling soda, you need to invoke memories of the good times spent with friends over an ice-cold cola. A good copywriter knows how to amplify the feelings that are already embedded in the readers' experience.

Don't "Sell" Savings

If you're using precious marketing real estate simply for chest-thumping about your low prices, you're doing it wrong. Research proves that asking customers to compare prices directly is a bad idea, but new research from Stanford University has revealed that selling "time" is far more effective than selling savings.[1] Jennifer Aaker, the lead researcher, sought to explain why companies like Miller would use a slogan such as "It's Miller Time!" As an inexpensive beer company, shouldn't it be promoting its reasonable prices instead? No. A person's experience with a product tends to foster feelings of personal connection with it. Referring to someone's time with a product typically leads to more favorable attitudes—and to more purchases.

Don't spend all your words in crunching numbers. Instead, speak to what really matters to your buyers—their time, their troubles, and their passions. We live in an era when people are busier than ever, and their time is more precious than their money. Once time is gone, it is gone forever. And that's why it's meaningful. We know that customers are willing to pay more for exceptional service, but you also need to understand that they're willing to pay more if you speak to them in a way that lets them know you value what they hope to achieve. Doing that is better than selling them on bottom-dollar prices.

Details Make the Difference

Whoever said, "Don't sweat the small stuff" wasn't a copywriter. In a fascinating piece of research from Carnegie Mellon University, researchers set up a free DVD trial program (remember DVDs?) that customers could register for. They tested it using two different phrases: "a $5 fee" and "a small $5 fee." Seems insignificant, but the second phrase increased sign-up rates by more than 20 percent.[2] It's a minor detail—a single word, actually—but it made a difference. Researchers discovered that the emphasis on the "small" fee made it far easier to deal with for conservative spenders, or as we call them here at StartupCamp.com, tightwads.

Take the time to measure, improve, and track the success of your words. Great writers today have no excuse for not testing their work, so make sure you're sweating the small stuff. Changing just one word might add a few zeros to your bottom line.

Always Opt for Action

Marketers love adjectives. In fact, in our last example it was an adjective, *small*, that made a big difference. But overuse of adjectives can be problematic. Putting too many of them in succession is like stuffing a mouth with marbles. So instead of relying on lots of adjectives, good copywriters opt for strong verbs. Instead of writing that you had a "slow, meticulous walk," just say you tiptoed. It's quicker, cleaner, and more likely to invoke feelings in the reader. I could tell you about my friend Brian, who is intelligent, hardworking, and really insightful. Big whoop. Everyone has a friend with those traits. Now what if I told you that my friend Brian founded a ten-million-dollar company and launched a top 100 podcast on iTunes? Much more impressive, right?

Some writers might not agree with this, but college kids will tell you: an admissions letter is one of the most stressful pieces of persuasive copy you can write. It is very much a piece of marketing—you're selling yourself to some person who decides if you're going to make it in or not. In a recent analysis of admission letters, as discussed by the Harvard MBA admissions director who read them for years, verbs beat out adjectives more often than not.[3] Why? Verbs are specific and are difficult to ignore, especially in a world where everybody describes themselves with the same trite adjectives.

You may not be a natural writer, but if you want to be an entrepreneur, you have to learn to write and like it. Remember, if you're bored while writing it, people will be bored when reading it.

☑ COMPLETE DAY #21

☐ REMEMBER

"If you're bored writing it, people will be bored reading it."
#LaunchYourDream

ASK

In what area is your writing the weakest, and what tangible steps can you take to improve?

☐ BELIEVE

I must find the time to find the right words.

☐ DO

Write a two-hundred-word sales pitch of your product to a fictitious customer. Amplify the feelings that are already there, focus on values rather than savings, and pare down your adjectives.

DAY 22

Every Post Has a Purpose

Estimated Reading Time: 10 Minutes

Let's start this day by having you answer two questions: First, where is the last great book you read? Is it lounging on your bookshelf at home, tucked into your backpack, maybe resting on your nightstand? Second, where's your cell phone? Is it slipped into your pocket, sitting on the arm of your couch, or charging quietly in the next room? I don't know the answer to either question, but I bet you located your phone more quickly than your book. And I also bet your phone was closer to you. Probably within reaching distance.

If you're reading this book in a public space—maybe a coffee shop or in your office—pause and look around. What do you see? Probably screens opened to social media. People are posting, commenting, scrolling, e-mailing, and taking selfies. It's a safe bet that wherever you are, you can see a few people staring into a phosphorescent light like an addicted drone.

Social media is heroin.

These realizations may reflect a sad reality for society, and you may lament how "kids these days" don't spend enough time outside. I won't disagree with you. But what is sad for society is great news for entrepreneurs like us. Because it means we have lots of customers who spend untold hours each day in the space where we will be marketing our start-ups. Modern society's addiction to technology makes it easier for starters to find and track customers. We know their location, their age, ethnicity, hobbies, and even marital status.

Even with all of this information at our fingertips, social media marketing can seem overwhelming. Twenty years ago social media didn't even exist. And obviously, then, the strategies and tactics to optimize your marketing in these spaces didn't exist. No one in Bill Clinton's administration was trying to figure out how to make a video go viral or leverage the power of promoted posts. The rate of change and innovation is far faster than it was twenty or thirty years ago. Nobody cares anymore if you have a degree in advertising because everything you learned when earning that degree is irrelevant by the time you graduate. As a result, today's marketers are under a unique level of pressure to keep up and produce results.

Today, marketing tactics and strategies are part of your daily regimen. They come and go in an ever-changing world. And your job is just to keep up with them, leverage them, and then recognize when they become obsolete.

Before I started writing this chapter, I read a few social media books. One was *The Art of Social Media*, by former Apple evangelist Guy Kawasaki.[1] The book was full of specific tactics, like avatar sizes and how to add spacing in Instagram posts. The insight was helpful and made a lot of sense. But Guy's book, published in 2014, will be at least partially irrelevant by the time the one you're reading is published. In fact, it was somewhat irrelevant by the time the ink dried. And it will be worthless in another five years.

All these realizations make social media marketing an overwhelming topic for entrepreneurs. But it doesn't need to be. Because while the tools we use are constantly changing, many basic marketing principles are timeless. That's why it is best to focus on the evergreen principles that make up the foundation of social marketing and then apply them to a social media world. By focusing on the following six principles, you'll be able to build a powerful brand that connects with customers for a fraction of the cost that your biggest competitors spend.

Do What You Do, and Do It Well

Here is one of the most liberating statements I'll make in this book: you don't have to engage every social media platform. It's okay if you aren't on the top fifteen networks, trying to keep up with every little innovation in each space. Choose the ones you are good at, and master those. I'm good on some social networks and not others. If a network arises that you think is particularly helpful in your industry and you can't seem to conquer it, outsource it. By paying for it, you'll also be forced to decide whether it is really worthwhile. If you deem it not worthwhile, let it go.

Speak to People the Way They Need to Hear It, Not the Way You Want to Say It

The best social media marketing—like all marketing—is based on empathy. Which is to say that it is unnatural. At our core, we humans are selfish beings, and leaders often struggle to cultivate selflessness in their work lives. When leaders speak empathetically, in ways that show they understand their listeners' needs and desires, those leaders rise above the rest. You must intentionally craft your words, posts, and marketing statements for your individual audience. Consider the words that trigger their emotions and appeal to their sensitivities. Be considerate enough to change your style to accommodate your customers' needs, culture, or beliefs. Thoughtfulness is the most powerful form of marketing. And speaking empathetically is not being inauthentic; it's being attentive.

Every Post Has a Purpose

Before you engage on a particular social network, determine the goals you hope to achieve there. Do you want to generate sales or clicks? Do you hope to build trust or educate? Then craft your posts with that purpose in mind. A purposeless post is a waste of energy.

Timing Matters

The *why* and *what* of your posts are most important, but the *when* must not be ignored. Research each platform to determine the best times to post there. Here's an interesting fact: 60 percent of the U.S. population lives on East Coast time. So if you're like me and live on the Pacific Coast, you'll need to schedule posts earlier than you might otherwise.

Be Real, but Not Too Real

Followers crave authenticity, transparency, and vulnerability. They are engaging in these social media spaces to be entertained and educated, but also to connect with real people. They want to know your story and be given a peek into your life. They want to know where you're winning and failing. At the same time, social media isn't the place to talk about your deepest, darkest secrets or to vomit about your personal life. Do not use social media to gossip about others, to tell us about the state of your marriage, or to post photos of the unexplained rash that showed up on your inner thigh. Treat your social media audience similarly to how you treat your actual friends. A friend who isn't authentic, transparent, or vulnerable isn't a good friend. And neither is a friend who lacks boundaries.

Embrace the Resistance

The anonymity and physical distance of social networks empowers bullies, and this is one of the top reasons people avoid it. Remember that resistance is just proof that you're standing for something. So you will likely encounter resistance, and when you do, here's how you handle it: with silence.

Over the past several years, I've received two death threats and probably ten thousand hateful comments online. I've gotten e-mails, physical mail, and even voicemails from people telling me how stupid, ignorant, disgusting, and appalling I am to them. While I've been told I have the skin of a rhinoceros, some of these vicious statements have left scars. Online influence is not for the faint of heart. I've learned the best response to such people is no response. Block them if you must, but do not engage people in the muck of their own misery. Use your silence as an instrument to purposefully avoid their poor character. If you give haters anything, they'll take everything.

—

When it comes to social media, live by the wisdom of a man who never lived to see it. Theodore Roosevelt said, "Do what you can, with what you have, where you are." No more and no less is required.

☑ COMPLETE DAY #22

☐  **REMEMBER**

"Speak up, even if your voice shakes."
#LaunchYourDream

☐ **ASK**

Which three social media networks do you navigate best?

☐  **BELIEVE**

I should speak to people how they need to hear it, not how I want to say it.

☐  **DO**

Create a consistent, yet realistic, posting schedule for your top three networks.

Hack to Huge

DAY 23

The Funnel

Estimated Reading Time: 9 Minutes

By the time I was twenty-three, I knew that I wanted to marry a certain kind of woman. I wanted to be with someone who loved God and wanted a family. Since I am so outgoing, I wanted to be with a woman who wasn't an extrovert because I didn't want to feel as though we were competing. I wanted a woman who was strong in areas where I was weak. (And I had always been attracted to Hispanic women, so I thought that characteristic would be a bonus.)

One day, I took my staff to a restaurant for an employee appreciation night and—boom—there she was. I had been friends with Veronica Vidaña and with her family since high school, but I had not seen her in five years. But she fit my entire checklist.

I wish I could say that I walked up, knelt down, and asked her to marry me before riding off into the sunset with her. But we all know that relationships don't work that way, except on the silver screen. My goal that night was not to convince her to marry me; I just wanted to get her to talk to me. I walked over and struck up a conversation. Then came step two: get her to hang out with me. I invited her to come rock climbing at the gym I owned. Next, I had to work to convince her to go on a date with me. (This admittedly took work since she wasn't interested at the time.) After our third date, I asked her if she would start a committed relationship with me. For some reason, she agreed. Our relationship continued for nine months until, on a gondola ride at Newport Beach Harbor, I asked her to marry me. Three months later, on Valentine's Day, Veronica and I had a small wedding with a few close friends.

I'm guessing you've heard stories like ours before. It's a pretty common progression. If we know that building relationships with friends and spouses takes so much time and intentionality, why then would we assume that building relationships with customers would be different?

Entrepreneurs should think about the buying process like the dating process. First, you need to determine what your perfect customer looks like. For the purpose of this exercise, you need to look beyond your target customers' demographics to the types of *behaviors* you'd hope to see.

For StartupCamp.com, the perfect customers look like this:

- They are regular readers of the StartupCamp.com blog.
- They follow me on social media.
- They are subscribers to my weekly e-mails.
- They are enrolled in one of our curriculums.
- They have graduated from the curriculum and have become alumni.
- They have referred a friend to the curriculum.
- Most important, they would have started a successful business.

Once you have listed your perfect customers' behaviors, you need to arrange them into an orderly chain of events in increasing degrees of commitment. This is known as your funnel. It becomes a visual representation of the process you hope to take your customers through over time—from the first conversation to your metaphoric wedding day.

Too often, I see companies attempting to turn a brand-new visitor into a loyal customer overnight. And while this does happen sometimes, it's not common. Instead, we should focus our efforts on a series of different rings of a funnel, each with its own unique marketing message and goal. Step by step by step, we move the customer through these rings until they naturally convert into a customer and then willingly become promoters of the product.

The StartupCamp.com funnel looks like this:

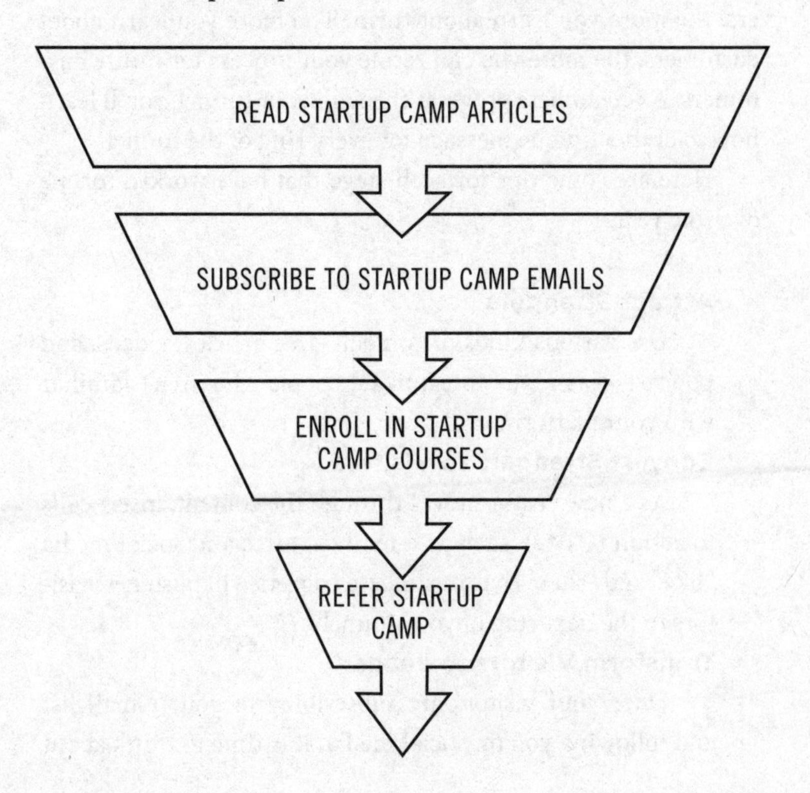

Too many entrepreneurs try to rush this process. They try to make a stranger become a customer overnight. Or they try to coerce a visitor to become a promoter without ever doing the work necessary to close the deal. Relationships simply don't work like this. And if you force the process to speed up beyond its natural pace, you'll often drive your customer out of the funnel completely. If you rush the funnel, you'll bust the funnel.

But even if you could speed up the process without breaking the system, great entrepreneurs wouldn't want to. They know that, as with the actual dating process, time is important for both parties. For the customer, the process builds trust. For the starter, the process solidifies the customer's commitment to you. And subsequently, the longer you interact with your customers, the more you learn about them. The more you learn about customers, the more you can refine your process for future customers. As customers progress through your funnel, you'll learn how to craft a unique message for every ring of the funnel.

Here are some tips for each stage that have worked for me over the years.

Attract Strangers

Use various kinds of content—free articles, videos, and podcasts—as a way to captivate people who aren't familiar with your platform.

Convert Strangers to Visitors

As a new visitor moves through the content, insert calls to action (CTAs), such as e-mail captures and social media "like" and "share" buttons. These triggers will push new visitors to the next ring of your funnel.

Transform Visitors to Leads

Once your visitors are subscribing to your e-mail list and following you on social media, it is time to think about conversion. Send e-mails to leads with a mix of free and premium content. But in the e-mail, preferably at the top, make a firm request to purchase your product or enroll in your program.

Close the Deal with Customers

Once the lead makes a purchase, congratulations! You have a new customer. But getting customers is different from keeping them. Now it is time to pull out the wow. Make sure your products exceed your customer's expectations.

Delighted Customers Make Great Promoters

For your start-up purposes, a promoter is any customer who is willing to refer a good friend to your product. If you impress customers with great products and then make a solid request, you are likely to transform them into promoters. And they are more likely to promote because you didn't rush the process. They've spent time with you, and you've earned their trust. And people will share brands they trust.

—

This all might sound like more trouble than it is worth. And maybe you think you're doing this anyway. What's the point of writing it out and formalizing your funnel? Those who have a system can hack a system. When you're able to track customer progression, you can evaluate what is and isn't working with precision. It's a mistake to assume that the language used to convince someone to move from the third ring to the fourth is the same that moves someone from the first to the second. It takes discipline to learn to speak to people in unique ways at each ring. (Understanding sales funnels can be difficult. To download a video overview of StartupCamp.com's funnel, visit StartupCamp.com/funnel.)

Once you understand how your customers operate at each stage of the process, you can spend revenue intentionally to feed your funnel at different stages. Your job is to figure out how to get people from each ring to the next. If you can get your funnel working and optimized, it will be a self-perpetuating sales machine.

☑ COMPLETE DAY #23

☐ REMEMBER

"When we focus on the process we focus on the proceeds."
#LaunchYourDream

☐ ASK

What are at least five qualities that comprise your perfect customer?

☐ BELIEVE

The stronger my process is, the bigger my profits will be.

☐ DO

Funnels can be complex. For practice, craft a five-ring funnel with your perfect customer at the center.

DAY 24

Smartcuts, Not Shortcuts

Estimated Reading Time: 8 Minutes

General Electric is one of the most successful businesses in the history of, well, business. My dad worked for that company for a quarter of a century, so in some way, I guess I owe it gratitude. It currently produces more than $120 billion in annual revenue. How did GE get to the top, and how has it stayed there? The firm constantly crunches the numbers, that's how.

GE developed a system called Six Sigma to determine product quality, process capability, customer satisfaction, and supply chain defects. The company uses these numbers to map its global performance.[1] Employees track and review these metrics as though it's their job. In fact, it is their job. And it is part of your job too.

If you operate blind, you'll stumble through the dark. Sadly, many entrepreneurs prefer to live with blindfolds on because tracking analytics can be stressful. After a post goes viral, watching your numbers orbit the stratosphere is fun. But when your online traffic tanks for no apparent reason, watching your numbers flatline can give you a mini-coronary. If entrepreneurs don't track their numbers, they avoid being responsible for them. So, many choose to ignore them altogether.

Your start-up may still succeed with an ostrich approach to business analytics, but it will be mostly by accident. You won't know when you experience an uptick in traffic or why. You will not know if you experience a drop-off in website visits—and if you do, you won't know why. You will have no idea if your conversion rate is growing or shrinking, and you won't know why it is happening. You'll have less stress, but you'll probably have less success too. When entrepreneurs fly blind, they usually crash.

So why do you need to embrace business analytics, and how can you track data without becoming a slave to it?

Every start-up should be collecting four types of information. *Quantitative data* includes user results, visits, and sales. These can be assembled easily into a spreadsheet and graphed. *Qualitative data* includes quality of service, website heat maps, customer complaints, and survey responses. *Comparative data* includes A-B testing results and conversion rates. And *competitive data* includes information gained from monitoring the activity of those who do what you do. If you're not monitoring your competitors, don't be surprised when you finish behind them.

Quantitative data is one of the most intimidating for entrepreneurs, but it is also one of the most important. Take time to assemble a dashboard where you can glance at your metrics in real time. (You'll find many dashboards available on the Internet. To see a free list of recommended tools, visit StartupCamp.com /tools.)

If you want to digest data quickly, it's imperative to have clear, intuitive data visualizations. But with far too many visual combinations available on the market (looking at you, Microsoft

Excel), it's easy to create excessively artistic dashboards that overwhelm the viewer. If you track everything, you'll end up tracking nothing, because it will feel overwhelming and you won't monitor it regularly.

Think about an airplane dashboard. Though it has more than one hundred indicator lights, dials, and gauges, pilots say they only focus on about a dozen. By focusing only on what's critical—fuel, altitude, speed—they streamline the process without overwhelming their brains. You should do the same. Choose a few metrics to monitor at first and add more over time. When you find an analytic isn't helpful, remove it from your dashboard. And resist the temptation to track everything.

Here are five types of data that most entrepreneurs put on their dashboard:

1. **Revenue and cash flow:** You can't afford not to track the financial health of your start-up.
2. **Advertising:** This helps you monitor the results of how you spend your money to move customers through your funnel.
3. **Social media:** Keep an eye on the health, engagement, and growth of your brand on social networks.
4. **Website analytics:** This data is critical for all modern businesses, but especially those who do most of their business online. Include visitor data as well as e-mail subscriptions and conversion rates.
5. **Customer data:** You need to know your annual customer value, retention rates, and attrition rates.

For StartupCamp.com, I use low-cost dashboard software that displays real-time metrics beautifully on my computer, iPhone, and office television. I look at it at least four times per day.

After two weeks of honing, here are the twelve dashboard metrics I settled on (numbers indicate the corresponding data type):

- Rolling thirty-day revenue (1)
- Daily revenue (1)
- Bank account balances (1)
- Weekly book sales (1)
- Advertising cost per acquisition (2)
- New followers across each social network (3)
- Daily web visitors (4)
- Daily website conversion (4)
- Weekly e-mail subscribers (4)
- Total paid students (5)
- New students today (5)
- Monthly student attrition rate (5)

Many entrepreneurs spend time creating a business plan for their organization to follow. However, that's just the first piece of success. The second is making sure your start-up is performing according to your plan's expectations. Your dashboard could do just that by automatically comparing the goals of your business plan with your actual, real-time results.

Once you see your results, you can make real-time adjustments. Growth hackers have so much information that they can literally turn up the volume knobs on what's working, kill what's not, and safely test new strategies without harming the company. If traffic is low, you can post another article. If sales are down, you can run an A-B test. If new social media followers are slowing, you can craft something creative to bring back the increase. When something isn't working, you won't freak out. Being an entrepreneur means being okay with a glimpse of something that is not working. Allowing anxieties to overwhelm you because of a few bad days isn't healthy. A snapshot doesn't show the whole picture, but the dashboard will help you assemble the complete portrait.

Humans are naturally on the lookout for shortcuts. We want to find faster, easier ways to get us from where we are to where we want to go. This drive for efficiency is woven into our DNA. But taking shortcuts isn't always the best way to do business. Quicker isn't better if, for example, your manufacturing process is sloppy and your product suffers. Instead, entrepreneurs need to learn to take *smartcuts*. While a shortcut will get you from point A to point B in less time and with less energy, a smartcut factors in characteristics like integrity, quality, and satisfaction. Tracking your business analytics is one of the essential smartcuts in an entrepreneur's toolbox.

If you fail to consider metrics, you'll have no way to measure your success or to increase your success. As management consultant Peter Drucker was known for quipping, "What gets measured gets managed."

☑ COMPLETE DAY #24

☐ REMEMBER

"Never guess when you can measure."

ASK

What are the top ten metrics you expect to drive your business?

☐ BELIEVE

I can't manage what I won't measure.

☐ DO

Review three dashboard software options, and decide which one works best for your start-up.

Keep Them Captivated

DAY 25

Unlearning Customer Service

Estimated Reading Time: 6 Minutes

If I gathered a group of young starters and asked them to name the most important element required to stay in business, most of them would say "profit." At first blush, the answer seems to make sense. If you don't make money, your business will go bankrupt. You can't advertise without money. You can't innovate without money. You can't manufacture without money. You can't eat without money. It's a compelling answer. But it's wrong.

The most important element required to stay in business is customers. Without your customers, you will have no profit. No purpose. No reason for your products to exist. Make no mistake; your customers pay your salary. Your family survives because your customers buy. You're free to take a vacation because your customers buy. You can pay for a movie ticket because your customers buy. You may write yourself a check at the end of the month, but your customers guarantee that it won't bounce.

Imagine that your office phone rings, and a customer

introduces herself on the other line. At that moment, the most important person in the world to you is that customer. Many entrepreneurs say they realize this, but they don't always act like it. That's why you'll hear entrepreneurs who are on the phone saying things like, "I'm sorry, but we're out of stock, and we don't know when we'll have more." Or "I'm sorry, but this is the best we can do right now." Or "I'm sorry, but our policy won't allow that." We despise hearing these statements when we are the customer, yet we use them with our customers all the time.

These types of phrases are perfectly acceptable in the world of customer service. And that is why entrepreneurs need to unlearn customer service and relearn customer obsession.

Shifting your perspective begins with shifting your framework. Customer service is a reactive discipline. These are the tactics employed when something has gone awry. Companies use customer service as a tool to put out fires and ease anger. They use it when a product has malfunctioned or when an expectation has not been met. Customer obsession, by contrast, is a proactive discipline. When a customer has reached the need for customer service, it is a sign that you're already failing. So at StartupCamp.com, I train my campers to ban customer service thinking from their businesses.

Here are five customer obsession principles every entrepreneur should live by.

Restore Respect

Speak to your customers the way you would want to be spoken to as a customer. This is the golden rule of start-ups.

Live Up to Your Commitments

If you make a promise, you should keep a promise. If you're forced to break it because of something outside your control, don't "even things up" with the customers. Go above and beyond to give them more than they would have received otherwise.

Answer Immediately

If your customer e-mails you a question or leaves a message on your voicemail, do not sit on it until answering is convenient. Since customer obsession calls for you to recognize that customers are more important than you are, you must work around the customer's schedule, not the other way around.

Elevate People Over Policies

Company policies are usually designed to serve companies, not customers. When a customer makes a request, do not reject it because of a policy. This tells them that you believe arbitrary words on a piece of paper are more important than their satisfaction.

Make No a Dirty Word

Your customer wants to hear you say yes. If you can't give them a yes immediately, then find a way to get them a yes eventually. If you tell your customers no, they will find someone who will tell them yes.

—

The key difference between customer service and customer obsession is that the former is rooted in procedures while the latter stems from feelings. We want to make sure our customers are convinced that we care about them more than we care about ourselves even *before* something goes wrong. When they feel that you care early, they'll be less inclined to make you work overtime to prove it later. When they feel that you understand them and that you are prepared to serve them, they'll work with you instead of against you to solve problems.

☑ COMPLETE DAY #25

☐ REMEMBER

"Treat your customers like they own you. Because they do."

—Mark Cuban

ASK

Think about an incredible customer service experience from your life. What lessons from that experience can you incorporate into your start-up?

BELIEVE

My family survives because my customer buys.

DO

In addition to the five customer obsession practices above, draft three more that are unique to your business.

DAY 26

Too Cheap Not to Keep

Estimated Reading Time: 10 Minutes

On the far side of our family farm, six apple trees are soaking up sunshine. If we take good care of those trees, they'll take good care of us. They'll give us a nearly endless supply of fruit to crunch into on lazy summer days, smother with peanut butter, and bake into pies. But even if we tend those trees with expert precision, a few mealy, brown, rotten apples will find their way onto our branches. Even the healthiest trees will have a few bad apples.

In the same way, you can follow every principle we've covered so far and even build a culture of customer obsession, but you'll still have some disgruntled customers along the way. I know entrepreneurs who treat unhappy customers like rotten apples. They throw them away or give them subtle hints that they should do business elsewhere. This frees up their time to tend to the healthier, happier ones. But such a strategy ignores a critical business principle: it is always less expensive to keep a current customer than attract a new one.

Depending on which industry you're in, recent research shows it will cost you anywhere from five to twenty-five times more to find a new customer and move them to point of sale than to keep an existing customer who is already in your funnel.[1] Customer retention is always cheaper than customer acquisition.

One way to shift your thinking on this is to start considering the *lifetime value* of a happy customer. For example, if someone signs up for a StartupCamp.com enrollment package valued at $99 per month and we keep them happy, they are worth $1,200 for that year. If we retain them, they may buy tickets to our annual StartupCamp Summit, purchase one of my books, and pick up a consulting session. As we prove our worth to them, they may refer a few friends to us, who in turn may follow the same trajectory. If they stay engaged for two or four or ten years, this single person's lifetime value may be equal to a six-figure profit.

If we bleed customers and lose them after only a few months, each customer may have a lifetime value of only a few hundred dollars. We can survive if we invest money in advertising to attract a lot of those customers. But we're eating into our profits by acquiring them. We might survive on two hundred of the first kind of customer—the lifetime customer—but we need around twenty thousand of the other kind.

The goal, then, is not to get a wide array of people spending a little bit of money, but to convince a select community of people to spend a lot of money. You should be investing at least as much money into keeping customers as you are into attracting new ones.

Every business is like a cup with a hole in its bottom. No matter how much water you add, the cup will always leak. If you stop adding water, your cup will run empty. If you add less water than you're leaking, your cup will run empty. Entrepreneurs must find ways to plug their leaks as much as possible while consistently adding water.

This analogy raises a critical question: How big is the hole in your cup? How fast are you losing existing customers? Since you are tracking your analytics, then you already know the answer to this by looking at your customer attrition and retention rates. Once you have the quantitative data on how big your leak is, then you need to couple it with the qualitative data about what is causing your leak. Why are people leaving? What reasons do they give for canceling a service or returning a product?

As of the time of this writing, StartupCamp.com has a 10 percent cancellation rate, meaning we lose one existing customer for every ten new customers we acquire. For my industry, that's a pretty small hole overall. I could sit back and celebrate that 90 percent of our customers are satisfied. But instead, I'm listening to why customers are canceling so that I can drive that number down. I am not satisfied knowing that 10 percent of my customers are dissatisfied and maybe even telling their friends about that dissatisfaction.

Once you know how big your leak is and why the leaks are occurring, here are two steps for increasing customer retention.

Empathize

Many of your dissatisfied customers are easier to please than you assume. Before attempting to help them, make sure they know you hear them. Listen to what they are saying before you rush in to fix the issue. If you don't let them blow off steam, you'll force them to build up steam.

After hearing them out, verbally agree with them. A three-word phrase that should always be on the tip of your tongue is, "Oh, that's horrible!" If your customer is disgusted, you should be too. If your customer is disappointed, you should be too. If your customer is enraged, you should be too. Make sure your customer knows that you feel what they feel, and don't offer them a bunch of lame excuses. By learning to empathize, you will remind customers that you are their teammate rather than their competitor. This attitude will decrease the chance that you'll provoke an argument as you search for a solution to their problem.

Offer Incentives

If the customer still decides to leave even after you've worked to resolve their problem, sweeten the deal. Make it as difficult as possible for them to take their business elsewhere. Ask the open-ended question, "What can we do to retain your business?" If they can't think of an answer, then begin offering options.

Fitness centers are often great at this strategy. You sign up for a monthly membership at $49 per month. But over time, you lose motivation or don't value the experience. So you phone them up and decide to cancel. What happens? They offer you a reduced rate of $29 per month, and suddenly the motivation returns. Before you know it, you're locked in for another twelve months. A stupid business owner would tabulate this scenario as a loss of $20 per month. A smart one would recognize that some money is better than no money at all.

A disappointed customer is just an opportunity for you to prove your value as a business. Give customers what they want, and if the problem was really your fault, do something that will blow their mind. Offer them a free month or an extra ticket or a credit toward their next purchase.

—

An angry customer turned into a raving fan often is more loyal than ever before. Never forget that customers ready to repeat their purchases are the most powerful business advantage out there. That means the value of fixing defects, making amends, correcting mistakes, and creating a memorable recovery is probably higher than you might assume. If you shrug off the upset customers, you're going to miss out on revenue and give them a negative story about your start-up that they can tell and retell into eternity (the power of word-of-mouth marketing in reverse).

Work hard to solve problems and increase customer retention, and you'll find, in the words of an ancient king, your cup will overfloweth.

☑ COMPLETE DAY #26

☐  **REMEMBER**

"It takes months to find a customer and only seconds to lose one."
#LaunchYourDream

☐  **ASK**

What do you anticipate being the most prominent cause of your start-up's leak?

☐ **BELIEVE**

It is less expensive for me to keep a customer than attract a new one.

☐ **DO**

Create your customer recovery system, including two to three offerings for a customer on the verge of leaving.

DAY 27

More Profitable

Estimated Reading Time: 8 Minutes

What's the worst part about flying? The cramped seats? Those insanely small bags of peanuts (assuming the airline you've chosen isn't too cheap to serve them)? The way your suitcase always seems to end up in a country you've never even visited? Let's just summarize all of our problems and say "airlines." If you ask frequent travelers for an airline nightmare story, they'll probably give you ten.

When you think of quality customer service, airlines don't usually come to mind. But Southwest has continued to be an innovator in this industry. The company is known for low-cost fares and flight crews that work hard to make trips enjoyable or even comedic. Additionally, it is one of the few airlines that has refused to charge customers for checking a bag or penalize them with change fees if they need to reschedule.

The Southwest approach was recently on display when a traveler was heading from Los Angeles to Denver to see his three-year-old grandson for the last time. The boy had been beaten into a coma by his mother's boyfriend and was being taken off life support that evening. The customer's wife called Southwest to book a last-minute fare, explaining the difficult situation. Thanks to heavy traffic, however, the man did not arrive at the gate until twelve minutes after the plane was scheduled to take off.

But the story did not have the sad ending you might expect. When the man arrived at the gate, he was stunned to find the pilot waiting for him. "They can't go anywhere without me, and I wasn't going anywhere without you," the pilot told him. "Now relax. We'll get you there. And again, I'm so sorry."[1]

In an era when too many companies worship the almighty dollar, Southwest Airlines has decided to place people over profit. It joins companies like Whole Foods, Chick-fil-A, Patagonia, In-N-Out Burger, and REI. These companies work to see customers as fellow humans made of flesh, emotions, and an often hurting heart.

A couple of years ago, I studied exceptional, standout companies with loyal customer bases and committed employees. I asked what motivated them to remain ruthlessly committed to their vision and seemingly impervious to compromise. Which beliefs drove them to do business the way they did? I discovered that the best companies in the modern marketplace are those that realize there is more to making money than just making money. And if you want your start-up to be a standout, you too need to live by the same principle: value people over profit.

A business that believes people matter works to give every employee respect, no matter where they fall on the organizational chart. It values every customer, no matter how much they spend. It treats everyone with fairness and respect. And—it wants to make money. I'm a capitalist, which is why my last book on this topic is titled *People Over Profit*, not *People Instead of Profit*.

Many "people matter" start-ups set a policy that attempts to give a response to every single customer who writes their company on social media. A response from a real person, not a robot. This is treating human beings like human beings. These start-ups don't have automated messages when you e-mail them. They include a number on their website that doesn't reroute callers to another country. And if they miss your call, no sweat. They'll get right back to you.

If you're in retail or manufacturing, then you need to consider where your materials are sourced. If you are getting your apparel from a sweatshop in Thailand to increase your profit margin, then you aren't living by this value. A start-up that believes people matter may choose to source locally or at least to research the ethics in its own supply chain.

Before I sold my stock in my previous e-commerce company, it sold T-shirts. All of its printed apparel was made with cotton that was woven in Los Angeles, near our offices. It wasn't the cheapest cotton, but it supported those who lived at our back door. Those who cut and sewed the garment or printed on the garment became our friends. I walked the facilities, met the manufacturers, and we verified that the products were made with the utmost ethical care. We refused to support a faceless manufacturer, even if it would save us money.

Most companies value only people who make them money or give them their money. But a start-up that believes people matter will recognize that people—all people—are intrinsically and equally valuable. They all have struggles, excitements, and joys. None should be forced to sacrifice their dignity or humanity. Everyone is worth loving, caring for, and serving well.

At first blush, this belief doesn't sound innovative. It is pretty simple. Almost too simple. This philosophy is more reminiscent of the values parents teach children than it is of a cutting-edge corporate sketch in the *Harvard Business Review*.

But people have struggled with this virtue since the beginning of time. Not to lie, not to manipulate or deceive, and not to mistreat those who have treated you poorly—these are behaviors humans struggle to resist. So maybe the simplicity and difficulty of this concept is also the secret to its power.

Don't be surprised if the entrepreneur inside of you is starting to recoil. This time-tested philosophy is countercultural and counterintuitive. It often rubs like sandpaper against basic business tendencies. That is what makes the belief as revolutionary as it is simplistic. Though this principle is rooted in old wisdom, it can empower you to forge new frontiers in the marketplace and in life. Even beyond business, this belief is a proven principle to living with purpose, generating greater success, and creating the world we all crave.

Interestingly, the idea that people matter has formed the cornerstones of some of the most successful leaders and organizations in marketplace history. When a business values people over profit, it ends up making more profit anyway. Of course, most of these companies don't use this phrase exactly. It doesn't appear in their company handbook, and isn't engraved in brass at the door of their headquarters. But the idea is present, animating everything from their marketing materials to employee appreciation to customer service commitments. If you commit to this idea at the very outset of your start-up, it can form the rudder to keep you on course no matter how large you grow.

Oh, and one point that also needs to be made. To be a start-up that cares about people, you also need to make sure you are treating yourself well. After all, you're a person too.

☑ COMPLETE DAY #27

☐ REMEMBER

"Valuing people over profit will always leave you more profit."

#LaunchYourDream

ASK

How do start-ups often struggle to value those they work with?

☐ BELIEVE

Valuing people over profit is more profitable too.

DO

Write a one-to two-paragraph, people-centric creed to guide how your start-up values vendors, employees, and customers. Your goal is to make it inspiring and almost poetic.

DAY 28

Culture Eats Strategy

Estimated Reading Time: 9 Minutes

Your company begins to have a culture when your company includes anyone other than you. This person doesn't need to work forty hours a week or have a comprehensive benefits package. It could be your spouse. A vendor. A freelancer. A web designer. A friend who has volunteered time. These people are part of your team. And if your team's morale fails, then your start-up is not far behind.

So don't be so focused on your bottom line that you forget to care for those around you. You are their leader, so you must ensure they are excited and cared for, not tired and underappreciated. Are your team members undercompensated or are they financially validated? Are they encouraged to think differently and dream big or do they check off a task list and punch a clock? Are they in the loop about the direction the organization is moving or do they operate on a need-to-know basis? Do they feel like cogs in a machine or like integral partners in pursuit of a greater mission?

You can have a well-oiled marketing machine, but if your

start-up's culture stinks, you're in trouble. You can have the best advertisements on the Internet, but if your people aren't happy, you're in trouble. You can have the most amazing products on the planet, but if your people aren't happy, you're in trouble. On the other hand, a happy team will cover a multitude of business sins. As Peter Drucker famously said, "Culture eats strategy for breakfast."

I've led a company with fifty employees, and I've led companies with no employees. The rules do not change. My team at StartupCamp is only five people right now, and not everyone works full-time. But every employee I hire still gets an onboarding package and a personal letter from me welcoming them to the team. They even get a welcome gift that aligns with our brand. I make it my business to make them feel appreciated and taken care of.

A common failing among entrepreneurs is that they spend so much time thinking about the outside of their business—branding, logos, ads, supply chains, product distribution—that they might stop paying attention to the inside. You cannot forget to cultivate a great corporate culture, to be the kind of company the best employees would be proud to work for.

If you want to evaluate the health of your start-up's culture, perform an audit. Ask anyone who works with you on a regular basis to answer these questions:

- Do you feel that I appreciate you?
- Do I maintain a high level of communication with every layer of our team?
- Do I encourage you to be yourself and work within your natural talents and passions?
- Do I provide ways for you to develop and grow and advance?

- Do I weigh you down with complex or meaningless rules and policies?
- Do you feel proud to be associated with our start-up?

If your team members matter, your team members *know* they matter.

If you want to see a company that values its team members, look no further than Clif Bar, maker of tasty treats made with high-quality natural ingredients. Founded in 1992, the company now has more than three hundred employees who rave about where they work. A few years ago, Clif Bar moved to a new set of digs complete with four wide-open gardens, a fleet of loaner bikes available for running errands, and a fitness center with a climbing wall, a yoga room, two massage rooms, and free access to five personal trainers and nutritionists. Employees get 2.5 hours of paid gym time per week.

Clif Bar's perks don't stop there. Every employee gets a $350 stipend for entering races and competitions and $1,000 per year for eco-conscious home improvements. Each week, there is a company-wide breakfast with free food where a Clif Bar fan letter is read. Employees can choose from several flexible work options to fit their unique schedules, and after seven years of service, they receive a six- to eight-week sabbatical. Oh, and if you love your golden retriever, don't worry. The office is dog friendly too. Do you think the Clif Bar team members know they matter? Exactly.

You don't have to have gobs of money to make team members feel they matter. One way to make sure to enhance your start-up's culture is to communicate well with potential employees during the hiring process. Too many people are hired by start-ups only to find out that they weren't given an accurate description by their employer. As time goes on, disparate responsibilities and expectations are tacked on. In a matter of months, employees end up way over their heads and swimming in frustration. When employees hand in their resignation letters, the starter is shocked. But they should have seen it coming.

At my previous company, I refused to hire anyone until we had drafted a position results description (PRD) outlining the job description and all the expectations for results and performance. I wanted to be honest about what each employee was being hired to do and what would be required of him or her. The potential employee would then agree to this PRD before being hired. With this, I hoped that no employee would look at my company and say, "When I was hired, I never knew this would be a part of my job" or "You hired me to do something else." When trust is high, everything works faster.

Being an entrepreneur often means being really cheap. Especially at the beginning of the launch phase, when you're operating on a shoestring budget. We can't afford not to be cheap. But when you hire people, you need to pay them what they are worth. In fact, you should find ways to pay your team members more than they are worth. And if you can't pay them as much as you wish, make it up to them in other ways. Give them more vacation time. Allow them to take half a day off on Friday. Throw your team regular parties. Take them out to lunch and pick up the check. If your team is underpaid, your start-up's morale will plummet. And your start-up won't be far behind.

Some start-ups believe culture is so important that they hire someone just to oversee it. They have a director of culture and community who is tasked with making sure that employees are happy, valued, and building strong relationships with each other. This person holds the team accountable to make sure the members live out their culture every day. This has always seemed like a good idea for any start-up after it begins hiring employees. But don't fool yourself into thinking that you can grow and remain committed to this value without someone who is doing it as part of their job.

Strive to be like Google, not like the IRS. Become the start-up everyone wants to work for. Become the start-up people would take a pay cut to work for. Become the start-up that team members miss when they are on vacation. If your company culture eats your strategy for breakfast, your start-up will eat the competition for dinner.

☑ COMPLETE DAY #28

☐ **REMEMBER**

"How you make team members feel about themselves says a lot about your leadership."
#LaunchYourDream

☐ **ASK**

What do you plan to do to make your start-up's culture extraordinary?

☐ **BELIEVE**

If my team members matter, my team members will *know* they matter.

☐  **DO**

Draft an onboarding process to use with your first new team member.

Beat the Barriers

DAY 29

A Learnable Skill

Estimated Reading Time: 8 Minutes

Normally, when Facebook wants to notify you of something, it sends an automated e-mail. You know it is serious when a real-live human being from Facebook headquarters calls your personal phone number. That's exactly what happened to me in February 2014.

The woman on the other end of the phone informed me that she was an event coordinator with the social media network and wanted to invite me to give a keynote address at the Facebook global marketing summit in San Francisco. I hadn't done much public speaking at the time, and certainly nothing of this caliber. The invitation was daunting, and I grew more nervous as she added details. I would give my speech to a crowd of two thousand Facebook global employees—in honor of the company's tenth anniversary—and my speech was to precede a keynote by the company's iconic founder, Mark Zuckerberg. Oh yeah, and I had only sixty days to prepare.

As the event coordinator continued to speak, a lump gathered in my throat and my stomach tightened. What did Facebook see in me that I didn't even see in myself? The invitation intimidated me; but in the moment, I recalled something I've often said to other entrepreneurs: "An entrepreneur often bites off more than he can chew, hoping that he will quickly learn how to chew it." I said yes before I had the chance to think about the implications.

Have you ever found yourself in a situation like this? An opportunity falls into your lap, and you wonder if you're prepared for it? Or you catch a big break, but the gap between what you know and what you need to know seems unbridgeable?

One of the scariest things for entrepreneurs is coming to know what we don't know. Maybe you need to know something about accounting, but you can't even work the calculator app on your phone. Or you wrote down the best practices for organizing your office, but you can't remember which pile of paper it is buried under. Perhaps you know you need to launch a blog, but you struggle even when writing an e-mail. Here's the good news: you can always learn what you don't know.

A friend of mine who is a successful businessman once told me, "If you're not willing to learn, no one can help you. But if you're determined to learn, no one can stop you." In the past decade, I have read more than two hundred books, taken an executive coaching course led by a psychotherapist, engaged with a millionaire mentor for three years, and even joined a few elite mastermind groups. Why? Because education is not optional for entrepreneurs.

Too many starters drop out of school to launch their business. While the traditional school system is an ineffective tool for most entrepreneurs, education is not. You must constantly be learning if you want to succeed as an entrepreneur. This doesn't mean paying hefty tuition to an Ivy League MBA program or even reading a thousand-page academic volume on economics. One of the easiest and best ways to educate yourself isn't reaching for an encyclopedia; it's reaching for a friend. People are deep reservoirs of acquired knowledge, and learning from those we know costs us nothing.

After Facebook contacted me, I phoned my friend Jon Acuff, a respected and successful public speaker. I offered to pay him to come to my home and spend two days training me in crafting a great speech. By the time John left, I had pages of notes and felt better prepared to write a killer speech.

Jon reminded me how perfectionism can often hamper the ability to craft a great talk. He said, "Ninety percent perfect and shared with the world always changes more lives than 100 percent perfect and stuck in your head." We often think of perfection as a laudable characteristic, but it can be a hindrance to our greatest achievements. Had I not spent time with Jon, I might have become paralyzed by the greatness of the task before me and unable to put my talk on paper. In the same way, you should make good use of your wisest friends to fill in the knowledge gaps that are holding you back.

It is important to accept that you don't need to be smarter to be a starter. Our whole lives we have been told that if we aren't prepared, we should not say yes. But entrepreneurs don't think this way. They often say yes to an opportunity before they know how to pull it off. In fact, saying yes is a great catalyst to motivate the learning process. The best motivation for me to write a talk that could slay a crowd was for me to agree to face them.

Yes has another interesting effect on us. Each time we accept an opportunity and then find a way to become successful, we make a deposit in the confidence bank. Over time, we begin to say yes more easily because we've come to believe that we can pull off just about anything. If you don't believe me, test it. Think of something you've been too afraid to say yes to and accept the challenge today. See if you don't get a boost of confidence when you pop out on the other side.

Sixty days after I accepted the Facebook invitation, I used the knowledge I had acquired from Jon and delivered a top-notch talk. In front of an audience of two thousand innovators in downtown San Francisco, I spoke on the topic "Dare to Change the World." And you know what? Preparing and giving the talk was the greatest learning experience of the entire ordeal. Sometimes entrepreneurs will learn *before* doing, but often they will learn *by* doing. But they must always be learning, no matter what.

☑ COMPLETE DAY #29

☐ REMEMBER

"Entrepreneurs learn by doing, not by learning to do."
#LaunchYourDream

☐ ASK

What is one area where you feel incompetent, and how is it stopping you from starting?

☐ BELIEVE

I can always learn what I don't know.

☐ DO

Identify one friend who is strong where you are weak in business. Contact them today to set up a meeting for the purpose of learning from them.

DAY 30

Mature Thinking

Estimated Reading Time: 9 Minutes

Congratulations—you have completed the first thirty days of the rest of your life. Graduating from StartupCamp drastically improves your chance of success. While entrepreneurs have a notoriously high failure rate, you won't be a part of this statistic. You have read this book, tapped into your passions, created a comprehensive business plan, and thought through every detail. You're going to take smartcuts I've learned over more than a dozen years of experience. You won't make the mistakes others fall into. Most people fail because they aren't prepared, but you are. You may be going into battle, but now you've been through boot camp.

But even if you don't face full-on failure, you'll still have to face difficulty. As you walk into the storm, prepare to get knocked down. The market can shift, your capital can dry up, the search engine algorithm can change, or the law can be altered by some goofball politician who hasn't run a business a day in his life. In the blink of an eye, a new technology can emerge and make your company or product obsolete. A critical employee can quit without notice; a vendor can run out of stock and wreck your supply chain; a disgruntled customer can make a full-time job out of trashing you online. When these problems arise, no one will be holding your hand. How will you remain strong when the storm rages? How will you withstand whatever comes your way?

The first step to overcoming problems is to anticipate them. The worst time to prepare yourself for a problem is when you're in the middle of it. So steady yourself in the calm seasons. Shore up your friendships. Save money for lean times. Get ready before you need to be. And consider this chapter your pre-problem preparation manual. These three principles will help you withstand whatever comes your way.

Problems Equal Progress

I started my first business with an assumption that I had to solve every problem by myself and immediately. As a driven, type-A, inexperienced leader, I could become enraged by any obstacle. They got in the way of my progress and could divert all my energy without notice. But over time, I learned what all entrepreneurs must accept: problems are unavoidable, and the way you choose to handle them is critical.

Small businesses are problem-creating machines, so the obstacles can become overwhelming. Everyone has a threshold of control. Some people can handle a certain amount of uncertainty in their lives or even a certain number of challenges before they start to shut down. Others have an expanded capacity to deal with problems immediately, fielding them like a shortstop on a baseball team. Knowing your capacity for dealing with difficulty and enlisting the help of your team to step in when you're getting overwhelmed is crucial.

Luckily, your capacity for solving problems can be expanded just by encountering them. And similarly to learning to play a new instrument, if you keep practicing, you'll improve. The number of hours you practice determines the level of preparation for facing problems. Similarly, with problem solving it's not how long you've been doing it, but how many problems you've solved that counts.

Failure Is a Gifted Instructor

Failure will teach you more than any college professor ever will. But both instructors have this in common: their capacity to teach you is directly related to your willingness to learn. Many entrepreneurs agree that difficult times provide lessons to be learned, but somehow knowing this doesn't change the way they operate. They melt down into a code-red alert when something goes wrong—and once it is over, they are so overcome with relief that they fail to reflect on the experience.

When difficulty first emerges, it is the questions you ask, not the actions you take, that make the difference. Don't ask, "Why is this happening to me?" Or "What did I do to deserve this?" Begin instead with, "What can I learn from this that will make me a better business leader, spouse, parent, friend?" Lean into the problem's lesson as you search for the problem's solution.

When difficulty dissipates, take time to reflect. Have a quick meeting with those who witnessed and helped resolve the conflict. Ask them what they learned and how the process could improve the business's attitudes and actions going forward. Failure becomes permanent only when you refuse to learn from it.

Success Is Often the Offspring of Failure

Albert Einstein once said, "Failure is success in progress." He was right. As you learn from failure, you grow through failure. Your start-up's policies get sharper; your vision gets clearer; your team moves quicker; your skin grows thicker. Failure also has a way of keeping the ego in line, and success is better achieved when the leader is humble.

Zach Cutler, a contributor to *Entrepreneur* magazine, said:

> Remaining down to earth and honest is a challenge in today's business world. When deal after deal is going through seamlessly and business is on a steep incline, it's easy to get a big head.
>
> With that, those experiencing constant success may even resort to dishonesty if it means not losing what they have. They become slaves to success and before realizing it, they'll do anything to stay on top, things they would never have imagined. Partnerships and friendships are ruined. Family conflicts abound. It's all downhill from there, maybe except for the bank account.
>
> Failure humbles us when we so desperately need to be humbled. It helps us remember where we came from and keeps us in check.[1]

If failure breeds humility and refinement and reflection and strength, then failure is really success in disguise.

—

As you launch your start-up, remember that any time you're attempting to add value, you will face difficulty. Problems are proof that you're innovating. Problems are proof that you're evolving and growing. This is the secret to success: your biggest breakthroughs in business will come from what you once thought were your greatest challenges. Problems are gifts. The trick is just learning which to take on, and how to solve them quickly.

I remember the conversations in early 2014 that led me to leave the comfort of my steady income at the e-commerce company I had founded. I second-guessed my impulse to bow out. And then I third- and fourth-guessed it. *Should I really be leaving, or should I fight to stay?* I felt as though I was starting over, and I wasn't sure I was capable of creating anything as impactful as my work had been. I had no plans and no ideas, just my passions and my family.

The day I left, a wave of fear crashed over me. I visited my best friend's house to vent: "I might need to borrow some money if I can't figure something out." He smiled and reminded me of who I was.

"Dale, you're an entrepreneur. You've been able to create beautiful things from nothing. Not just once, but many times," he said. "This fear is temporary. And this fear is where you thrive. Don't let it lie to you. Take a few days off, and on Monday, create your new life."

That Monday, I created StartupCamp.

Today, we conclude our thirty-day journey from fear to freedom. This is a big day not only for you but also for me. Because you are proof that we can overcome difficulty. You are proof that problems are temporary. You are proof that failure is really success. You are proof that anyone can create a business, movement, or idea that will change the world.

Get out there and live your dreams.

☑ COMPLETE DAY #30

☐ REMEMBER

"Never get so busy making a living that you forget to make a life."

#LaunchYourDream

☐ ASK

What has caused you to quit in the past, and how can you prevent it from repeating itself?

☐ BELIEVE

Just because I stumble doesn't mean I have to stop. I will finish.

☐ DO

Go launch your business.

Having It All

Estimated Reading Time: 7 Minutes

The Atlantic inspired a national conversation a few years ago when it published a cover story titled "Why Women Still Can't Have It All." The article was written by Anne-Marie Slaughter, a former director at the U.S. State Department and dean of Princeton University's Woodrow Wilson School of Public and International Affairs, who had briefly left her job in government to care for her family. Contrary to the assertions of modern feminism, Slaughter argued, most women in America *can't* have it all—a career, a marriage, children, a social life. At least not all at once.

Jobs often make it difficult for parents to work, and many homeplace expectations are placed on women and not men. Some expectations—particularly those related to children's biological requirements of their mothers—can't be fulfilled by men. In addition, Slaughter said, every human being has certain constraints and must choose between competing options. Unless something changes in the American culture and economy, the only women who can have it all are the "superhuman, rich or self-employed."[1]

While someone might dispute Slaughter's conclusion—and many have—the basic question is sound. And it's bigger than a single gender. Every entrepreneur, man or woman, should wrestle with the question, "Can you have it all?"

The answer depends on how you define *all*, of course. My definition is not about having all things at all times for all seasons in all settings. It means fostering a holistically healthy life—emotionally, financially, socially, physically, and with your family. Most people are devoted to cultivating health in a few areas of life but not others.

For the entrepreneur, career often trumps all—at least in the initial phases of the start-up. This view can be detrimental because, even though the average age of an entrepreneur is forty,[2] many believe the average will drop rapidly in the coming years. The Internet has made it possible for younger people in their twenties and thirties to start businesses too. This means that starters run the risk of delaying marriage and family—or avoiding them altogether—because they are too consumed with launching and leading their businesses.

Now, there is nothing wrong with people who *want* to be single. But it is tragic when people desire marriage and a family, but nevertheless live alone. I can't count the number of entrepreneurs I've met who have reached age forty or fifty only to realize that they were more committed to work than promoting a holistically healthy life. The worst failure in life is in wanting to get married and have a family, having the ability to do so, but not building the margin for it to occur.

And don't assume that decisions about marriage and family are incidental to work. In fact, they are integrated. Entrepreneurs with supportive spouses and families who are willing to brainstorm creative solutions so they can live their dreams are far more likely to succeed. That's why Sheryl Sandberg, COO of Facebook, said, "The most important career decision you're going to make is whether or not you have a life partner and who that partner is."[3]

A problem of modern society is that it heavily emphasizes marketplace success. If you have a healthy marriage, few people are going to pat you on the back or take you out to a nice meal to celebrate. But they probably will if you sign a million-dollar deal or sell your company for a handsome profit. When you succeed in work, everyone stands on the sidelines and celebrates, pushing you to work harder and faster to re-create the high. It's easy to forget to start a family.

Of course, a family is not the only thing you should be mindful about. Don't eat greasy food until you can't walk and then refuse to go to the gym so you can finish typing up sales reports. Don't repeatedly tell your friends no when they invite you for a weekend away—they may finally stop asking. Start prioritizing the most important people and parts of your life now.

—

I walk through the sliding glass door that opens to the backyard behind our farmhouse just before sundown. Veronica is holding our daughter Aria's hand, just as I dreamed. I'm carrying our newborn son, Honor, in my arms—a reminder that dreams live and breathe and grow as we do. A group of our closest friends have come over to sit around the fire pit we've just finished building. Their laughter greets me as I join them around the roaring flames. My friends won't be able to stay too late because it's Saturday, and my family of four will rise early tomorrow to worship with our church community. The sun is setting behind the Cascade Mountains, scattering a purplish hue across the horizon, and a thought nearly knocks me down: *Having it all must be possible. Because I have it all.*

—

Your ultimate goal as an entrepreneur is not to have a successful start-up; your ultimate goal is to live a successful life. Your goal is to have it all. If your start-up is successful and your health is poor, you don't have it all. If your start-up is successful but your reputation is abysmal, you don't have it all. If your start-up is successful but your spiritual life is absent, you don't have it all. If your start-up is successful but your friends barely know you, you don't have it all. If your start-up is successful but your family is falling apart, you aren't successful.

The fire's lights are flickering in my wife's eyes as I turn back and peer into the windows of our living room. I can see an item that I inherited from my grandmother's house resting on an end table. It's an inspirational key hook that used to hang on her wall, and it's one of the only items I took from her house after she passed. When I was a child, I would stare at that key hook and ponder the phrase stamped upon it. As I grew to an adult, its message haunted me. And it still does. The words have guided me, and my family, on our journey through life. It may be the best piece of advice for any entrepreneur who wants to have it all:

Don't get so busy making a living that you forget to make a life.

Acknowledgments

Jesus
You've given me freedom, power, and authority. May I use it for your will, not mine.

Dad
You've been there through thick and thin, easy and difficult, and rich or poor. Thank you.

Carol
Thank you for filling the void in our family. It goes deeper than you realize.

Johnny and Cindy
I couldn't do this without the woman you raised. Thank you.

Matthew
God made us brothers for a reason; let's continue to find out why.

Aaron and Jen
There are very few people like you. Your friendship makes our family better, smarter, and closer to God.

Matt
I wouldn't be the man I am today without you. Thank you for the power.

Brady
My longest friend and biggest supporter. Thank you.

Jonathan
You're a wizard with words. Thank you for helping me write this book.

Chris
Thanks for always answering the phone. It's been an outlet for my dreams.

Notes

0: You Were Made for This

1. The full story is recounted in my previous book, *People Over Profit: Break the System, Live with Purpose, Be More Successful* (Nashville: Thomas Nelson, 2015).
2. Henry Cloud and John Townsend, *Boundaries with Kids: When to Say Yes, How to Say No to Take Control of Your Life* (Grand Rapids: Zondervan, 2001), 72.
3. Amy Adkins, "Most U.S. Employees Not Engaged Despite Gains," Gallup, January 28, 2015, www.gallup.com/poll/181289/majority-employees-not-engaged-despite-gains-2014.aspx.

Day 1: Primed with Passion

1. "Steve Jobs v Bill Gates: The Biggest Technology Rivals in History: In Pictures," *Telegraph*, www.telegraph.co.uk/technology/news/11364756/Technologys-biggest-rivalries-in-pictures.html?image=7.

Day 2: Calm in the Storm

1. Sangeeta Bharagwaj, "Many Potential Entrepreneurs Aren't Taking the Plunge," Gallup, February 18, 2015, www.gallup.com/businessjournal/181592/potential-entrepreneurs-aren-taking-plunge.aspx.
2. Ibid.

3. As quoted in Jessica Stillman, "How Amazon's Jeff Bezos Made One of the Toughest Decisions of His Career," *Inc.*, June 13, 2016, www.inc.com/jessica-stillman/jeff-bezos-this-is-how-to-avoid-regret.html.

Day 3: Personal Preparation

1. Steve Maraboli, *Unapologetically You: Reflections on Life and the Human Experience* (Port Washington, NY: A Better Today Publishing, 2013), 45.

Day 4: A Ship That Won't Sail

1. Amanda Neville, "Why Partnership Is Harder than Marriage," *Forbes*, March 1, 2013, www.forbes.com/sites/amandaneville/2013/03/01/why-partnership-is-harder-than-marriage/#5e293baf5289.

Day 5: An Irresistible Idea

1. Vivek Wadhwa, "How Entrepreneurs Come Up with Great Ideas," *Wall Street Journal*, April 29, 2013, www.wsj.com/articles/SB10001424127887324445904578283792526004684.
2. Richard Watson, "Why Good Ideas Go Bad," *Fast Company*, January 11, 2011, www.fastcompany.com/1718105/why-good-ideas-go-bad.
3. Brian Hamilton, "What Makes for a Really Good Business Idea," *Inc.*, www.inc.com/brian-hamilton/what-makes-for-a-good-business-idea.html.
4. Brandon Watts, "How Timing Can Make or Break a Startup," *Fast Company*, September 18, 2015, www.fastcompany.com/3051201/hit-the-ground-running/how-timing-can-make-or-break-a-startup.

Day 6: A Three-Part Foundation

1. Dave Ramsey, *EntreLeadership: 20 Years of Practical Business Wisdom from the Trenches* (New York: Howard, 2011), 27.

2. Steven Cox, "The North Star Guide to Your Startup: Core Values," *Entrepreneur*, April 24, 2014, www.entrepreneur.com/article/233323.

Day 7: A Business Doesn't Happen by Accident

1. Jeff Haden, "How to Write a Great Business Plan: Key Concepts," *Inc.*, April 1, 2015, www.inc.com/jeff-haden/how-to-write-a-great-business-plan-key-concepts.html.
2. Mark Henricks, "Do You Really Need a Business Plan?" *Entrepreneur*, December 2008, www.entrepreneur.com/article/198618.

Day 8: Whyology

1. Brian Hamilton, "What Makes for a Really Good Business Idea?" *Inc.*, January 10, 2014, www.inc.com/brian-hamilton/what-makes-for-a-good-business-idea.html.

Day 9: Brand School

1. "7 Most Expensive Logos in the World," *Think Marketing*, October 27, 2015, https://thinkmarketingmagazine.com/7-most-expensive-logos-world/.
2. Tom Peters, "The Brand Called You," *Fast Company*, August 31, 1997, www.fastcompany.com/28905/brand-called-you.

Day 13: Brains and Beauty

1. Neal Ungerleider, "Eyetracking and the Neuroscience of Good Web Design," *Fast Company*, October 17, 2013, www.fastcompany.com/3019886/buyology/eyetracking-and-the-neuroscience-of-good-web-design.
2. E. Silence et al., "Guidelines for Developing Trust in Health Websites" (paper on the proceedings of the 14th international conference on World Wide Web, WWW 2005, Chiba, Japan), www.conference.org/2005a/cdrom/docs/p1026.pdf.
3. Gitte Lindgaard et al., "Attention Web Designers: You Have 50 Milliseconds to Make a Good First Impression!" *Behaviour &*

Information Technology 25, no. 2 (2006), www.tandfonline.com /doi/abs/10.1080/01449290500330448.

4. Antoine de Saint-Exupéry, *Wind, Sand and Stars*, trans. Lewis Galantiere (1939; repr., New York: Harcourt, 2002), 42.

Day 14: Making It Legal

1. Eriq Gardner, "That's Hot: Paris Hilton Settles Hallmark Lawsuit," Reuters, www.reuters.com/article/us-hilton-idUSTRE68Q04Z2010 0927.
2. These definitions are taken from the Internal Revenue Service, 2015.

Day 15: A Small Leak Sinks Big Ships

1. Dave Ramsey, *Financial Peace Revisited* (New York: Viking, 2003), 20.
2. Dennis Jacobe, "One-Third of U.S. Small-Business Owners Feel Debt Burden," Gallup, May 16, 2012, www.gallup.com/poll /154664/one-third-small-business-owners-feel-debt-burden.aspx.

Day 16: Money in Your Sleep

1. Michael Simmons, "Is the 70-Hour Work Week Worth the Sacrifice?" *Forbes*, May 13, 2013, www.forbes.com/sites/michael simmons/2013/05/13/is-the-70-hour-work-week-worth-the -sacrifice/#3f5db0977943.

Day 17: Once in a Lifetime

1. Elaine Wong, "The Most Memorable Product Launches of 2010," *Forbes*, December 2010, www.forbes.com/2010/12/03/most
1. \-memorable-products-leadership-cmo-network.html.
2. Laurie Burkitt, "Brand Flops: Ford, GE, Coca-Cola Know Hype Can Hurt New Products," *Forbes*, March 2010, www.forbes.com /2010/03/31/brand-flops-apple-ford-pepsi-coors-cmo-network -brand-fail.html.
3. Joan Schneider and Julie Hall, "Why Most Product Launches Fail," *Harvard Business Review*, April 2011, https://hbr.org/2011 /04/why-most-product-launches-fail/ar/1.

4. Quoted in Barbara Thau, "The Five Biggest Reasons Why Consumer Products Fail," *Forbes*, June 3, 2014, www.forbes.com/sites/barbarathau/2014/06/03/the-five-biggest-reasons-why-consumer-products-fail-according-to-a-retail-insider/#6e5abc35905e.

Day 18: Building Smart into Your Start

1. Geoffrey James, "6 Emotions That Make Customers Buy," *Inc.*, February 2012, www.inc.com/geoffrey-james/6-emotions-that-make-customers-buy.html.
2. Joan Schneider and Julie Hall, "Why Most Product Launches Fail," *Harvard Business Review*, April 2011, https://hbr.org/2011/04/why-most-product-launches-fail/ar/1.

Day 19: A Talkable Experience

1. Kimberly Whitler, "Why Word of Mouth Marketing Is the Most Important Social Media," *Forbes*, July 17, 2014, www.forbes.com/sites/kimberlywhitler/2014/07/17/why-word-of-mouth-marketing-is-the-most-important-social-media/#5c42365c7a77.
2. Ibid.
3. I'd like to say that I came up with these terms, but they are quite common in business literature. A good article on this topic is Kimberly Whitler's "Why Word of Mouth Marketing Is the Most Important Social Media" at Forbes.com. I'm indebted to her for articulating this principle (www.forbes.com/sites/kimberlywhitler/2014/07/17/why-word-of-mouth-marketing-is-the-most-important-social-media/#73543cbd7a77).

Day 20: You're Not the Hero

1. See Carmine Gallo, "Mac 1984: Steve Jobs Revolutionizes the Art of Corporate Storytelling," *Forbes*, January 24, 2014, www.forbes.com/sites/carminegallo/2014/01/24/mac-1984-steve-jobs-revolutionizes-the-art-of-corporate-storytelling/#49833de67b2b.

2. Rodger Dean Duncan, "Tap the Power of Storytelling," *Forbes*, January 4, 2014, www.forbes.com/sites/rodgerdeanduncan/2014/01/04/tap-the-power-of-storytelling/#4da7106838cf.
3. Christopher Booker, *The Seven Basic Plots: Why We Tell Stories* (London: Continuum, 2004).
4. Donald Miller often notes that his inspiration for this idea came from communication guru Nancy Duarte. See her post "Great Presentations: The Audience Is the Hero" at www.duarte.com/great-presentations-the-audience-is-the-hero/.

Day 21: Wordsmith Wonders

1. Alice LaPlante, "Jennifer Aaker: The Happiness-Time Connection," Stanford Graduate School of Business, March 1, 2009, www.gsb.stanford.edu/insights/jennifer-aaker-happiness-time-connection.
2. Michael D. Smith and Rahul Telang, "Competing with Free: The Impact of Movie Broadcasts on DVD Sales and Internet Piracy," *MIS Quarterly*, June 2009, www.heinz.cmu.edu/~rtelang/SmithTelang.pdf.
3. Melissa Korn, "Harvard Business School? You'll Go Through Her First," *Wall Street Journal*, March 1, 2012, www.wsj.com/articles/SB10001424052970203833004577251490098811270.

Day 22: Every Post Has a Purpose

1. Guy Kawasaki and Peg Fitzpatrick, *The Art of Social Media: Power Tips for Power Users* (New York: Penguin, 2014).

Day 24: Smartcuts, Not Shortcuts

1. Philip Kim, "GE and the Culture of Analytics," *MIT Sloan Management Review*, January 27, 2014, http://sloanreview.mit.edu/article/ge-and-the-culture-of-analytics/.

Day 26: Too Cheap Not to Keep

1. Amy Gallo, "The Value of Keeping the Right Customers," *Harvard Business Review*, October 29, 2014, https://hbr.org/2014/10/the-value-of-keeping-the-right-customers/.

Day 27: More Profitable

1. William Lee Adams, "Hero Pilot Pulls Out the Stops to Help Grandpa Reach Funeral," *Time*, January 13, 2011, http://newsfeed.time.com/2011/01/13pilot-who-cares-the-most-heartwarming-airline-story-of-2011/.

Day 30: Mature Thinking

1. Zach Cutler, "Failure Is the Seed of Growth and Success," *Entrepreneur*, November 6, 2014, www.entrepreneur.com/article/239360.

+: Having It All

1. Anne-Marie Slaughter, "Why Women Can't Have It All," *Atlantic*, July/August 2012, www.theatlantic.com/magazine/archive/2012/07/why-women-still-cant-have-it-all/309020/.
2. George Deeb, "Age Really Is Just a Number When It Comes to Entrepreneurial Success," *Entrepreneur*, July 14, 2014, www.entrepreneur.com/article/235357.
3. Sheryl Sandberg, "Facebook COO Sandberg: The Women of My Generation Blew It, So Equality Is Up to You, Graduates," *Business Insider*, May 18, 2011, www.businessinsider.com/facebook-coo-sandberg-the-women-of-my-generation-blew-it-so-equality-is-up-to-you-graduates-2011-5.

About the Author

Dale Partridge is a serial entrepreneur, a *Wall Street Journal* bestselling author, and the founder of StartupCamp.com. Best known for his peculiar balance of family and business, Dale has over 1,000,000 followers on social media and 300,000 loyal readers of his blog. He is also a prominent influencer on the topics of entrepreneurship, branding, success, and leadership.

He is a trusted advisor to Facebook, Adobe, Ritz-Carlton, Chick-fil-A, and Panasonic. Dale has also been featured in various business publications, including MSNBC, Fox News, NBC, *Inc.* magazine, *Fast Company*, Mashable, MSN Money, *Forbes*, *The Today Show*, *Good Morning America*, *Los Angeles Times*, and the cover of *Entrepreneur* magazine. He resides with his wife, Veronica, and their children on a small farm in Bend, Oregon.

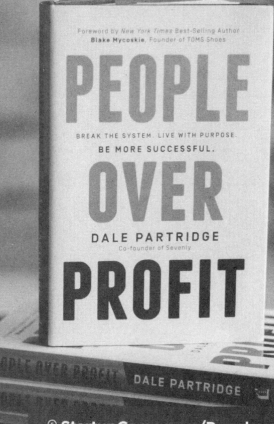